DAEDALUS HOWELL

AltWeekly Awards
Food Writing/Criticism, First Place

National Newspaper Association
Best Humorous Column

"Howell is connoisseur of both wine and words... If you've missed any of Howell's brilliantly self-deprecating, wine-soaked columns, or simply want to find them all under one roof, buy the book."

– Sonoma Magazine

I Heart Sonoma: How to Live & Drink in Wine Country

Direct reprint queries to:
FMRL P.O. Box 5124 Berkeley CA 94705 or FMRL.com.

ISBN-10: 0967100135
ISBN-13: 978-0967100135
Library of Congress Control Number 2011945828

Cover design by Sean Monroe, SeanMonroe.com. Cover photo courtesy of Digital Paws Inc.

Versions of these works have been published in the *Sonoma Index-Tribune*, *Sonoma Magazine*, *Sonoma Valley Sun* and the *North Bay Bohemian*.

The author gratefully acknowledges the contributions of his editors, among them David Bolling, Gretchen Giles, Bill Hoban, Marty Olmstead, Tim Omarzu and Ray Sikorski and Tim Zahner. Additional editing for this edition by Hiya Swanhuyser, Dmitra Smith and Dennis Ferguson.

The majority of these works were written under the influence of wine, which may account for the occasional forays into lies, fraud, and scandal.

Read Daedalus Howell's blog at DHowell.com.

I HEART SONOMA
How to Live & Drink in Wine Country

Selected Columns

By Daedalus Howell

FMRL
Berkeley, California

Contents

I HEART SONOMA
How to Live & Drink in Wine Country

Selected Columns

By Daedalus Howell

Author's Note

It's tempting to sum up a collection of columns like this particular one as some sort of "vintner's blend" or "columnist's cuvée." That would just be clever. Too clever. And untrue. This book is a valentine – a mash note to Sonoma, California – that pastoral pleasure dome just north of San Francisco.

Sonoma makes the concept of "Wine Country" seem like it should have its own flag. Actually, it did have its own flag, for about a month in 1846 thanks to the Bear Flag Revolt. Albeit, the cads in charge couldn't be bothered to form a provisional government so it soon foundered. I suspect wine was involved. Wine is always involved in the doings (and undoings) of Sonoma.

I'd like to think that Sonoma and I met at a time when we were both redefining ourselves, if not each other, like dormies in college or some other form of infinite regress. The valley was bubbling into national consciousness for its wine and epicurea just as I was winning my first national awards for writing about it. The accolades, however, were just the happy byproduct of a personal metamorphosis that Sonoma wholly made possible.

You see, I wrote these columns (and a couple hundred more that are fermenting elsewhere) during a period in my life when I had all but lost my voice as a writer. Or, perhaps

I hadn't altogether honed it. The point is, Sonoma and its unusually robust newspaper trade, allowed me to rebuild myself, word by word, in full view of a loyal and forgiving readership. I arrived broke and broken and departed not quite as broke and with a career reignited where once it was corked.

Given the environs, personalities and splendid peccadillos that define Sonoma, this was perhaps easier than I let on. Though the writing might have sometimes been labored, the inspiration flowed like wine (and other, equally intoxicating similes). There are few places on earth that one can appreciate both "through a wine glass, darkly" and rosé tinted glasses. Sonoma is one of them. There are many reasons to love Sonoma and nearly as many not to, depending on how much wine is left in the bottle. What follows are the reasons I *heart* Sonoma.

– Daedalus Howell
Oakland, California
2012

*For the Press Club
with special thanks to Flash
and the Contessa*

I, Sonoman – An Introduction

I didn't so much arrive in Sonoma, California, as end up here: I was on assignment, the assignment was canceled and so was my flight home. Well, at least, that's one story I tell people. I have other versions but this is the most succinctly shared between sips of wine.

Friends and family often observe to me that "Moving to Sonoma was one of the best decisions you've ever made." Though I'd love to take credit for having a prescient sense of my future happiness and success through choice of town, it's really the vicissitudes of the *writing life* that should get the nod.

This Fall, Sonoma and I will celebrate our five year anniversary together. Apparently it's our "silverware" anniversary – an upgrade, I understand, from what was once traditionally the "wood" anniversary. Though I did have my heart set on monogrammed chopsticks, I will honor the occasion by using silverware on some of Sonoma's award-winning epicurea whilst reflecting upon our years as citizen and city.

It's been a good match, and by that I don't mean pairing. I mean it's been a knock-down drag-out tussle for total domination over the other. Thus far, Sonoma is winning. It has taken a louche media burnout and reformed him into a pillar of the community. A pillar in the "Lot's wife" sense of the word, but a pillar nonetheless. In the past five years, Sonoma has given me everything and more: A career reboot, a wife, a child, and an upside-down mortgage – a keepsake I'll surely cherish for at least 30 years.*

Of course, I managed to get the sequence out of order. Retiring to the place where one vacations is the coda to the American dream and had I not been asleep at the wheel of my lifestyle choices I would certainly have chosen Sonoma as the place to lay the bullion of my Golden Years. I'd be in Heaven – in fact, I'd forfeit my place in Heaven just to stay in Sonoma, perhaps reincarnated as a vineyard dog or a board member of a non-profit organization.

However, I'm far from retirement and given Sonoma's natural beauty, beloved community, and gustatory gravitas, all other places on Earth now pale. Moreover, I'm getting used to it. Instead of vacations, I now have regular reality checks. Given the choice of visiting an amusement park or a business park, I'll choose the latter. A cul de sac of beige buildings hemmed with xeriscape is how I achieve perspective. I eat at national dining chains to remind myself how America actually tastes. If my hotel window doesn't have a view of a strip mall I change rooms. When you're a spoiled Sonoman, this passes as asceticism.

For prospective spoiled Sonomans, be you a retiree, a visitor or an accidental transplant, permit me to disabuse you of the five most common misperceptions about Sonoma.

1.) "Sonoma" is Miwok for "Napa-lite." Despite what linguists familiar with Native American tongues insist from their side of the border, according to author Jack London, "Sonoma" means "Valley of the Moon." Albeit, London's source was a bottle of whiskey.

2.) Sonoma offers wine cave spelunking. This is only partially true. Wine caves are generally laid out horizontally rather than vertically, which makes navigating them (and gravity) more intuitive. That said, after an in-cave wine tasting, some imbibers have been known to end up horizontal, creating the illusion of scaling a cave wall when one regards the floor at a 90-degree angle. Note to marketing departments: The addition of souvenir carabiners could add to the illusion.

3.) Getting married in a winery is romantic. Yes, for everyone except the winery staff. Since the salary for the in-house event coordinator takes up the entire event support budget, the winery's tasting room personnel are often drawn into the fold. To wit, your daughter may not have a world-class sommelier pairing wines with her nuptial nibbles, though the 30-something bottle jockey with a degree in philosophy and encyclopedic knowledge of *Star Wars* will do in a pinch. Mazel Tov!

4.) You can't judge a wine by its label. True, but you can judge a label by its wine. During the first glass, opinions run the full gamut – from "Hmm" to "Uh-huh." The second glass of wine leads to more in-depth label observations like "Hey, this bottle has a label on it." By the third glass, label critiques are often characterized by proclamations of "I love you, man" and "Let's get another bottle of – wait – what's it say on the label?"

5.) Sonoma's winery owners are filthy rich. Well, winery owners *used* to be filthy rich but, as the adage goes, to make a million in wine, start with ten million. Wine is largely a labor of love. And a tax shelter. The trick is getting the owners to "write off" a bottle in your presence. I've written off many a bottle since moving to Sonoma and a few have even written back.

Another point to consider when visiting Sonoma is one's wardrobe. Sonoma is like a masquerade ball, wherein everyone is disguised in cargo shorts and goatees – at least on the weekends when promenading the Historic Sonoma Plaza.

If you're not in need of camouflaging yourself as a local, your sartorial options are wide open. As most who have experienced the mercurial weather of the North Bay will attest, the smart money is on "layers." In Sonoma, not only should you wear layers, those layers should be dark and absorbent and made of black terrycloth. Just wear a towel. Even if you don't spill wine on yourself, someone else will. There's a word for this in philosophy (ask your "sommelier.") Inasmuch as one should never wear white after Labor Day, one should especially not in a tasting room, unless you "Wanna look like a tampon," as a tasting room manager once colorfully put it.

Please note: white wine may assist in the removal of red wine stains, but red wine does not remove white wine stains so much as make them red wine stains. If you get this procedure out of order, a vicious cycle ensues which will not end until your tab gets closed. Until then, please know I'm available to assist with emptying the bottles. It might not be the best decision you ever made, but chances are you won't remember it.

I've since short-sold the joint.

Napa is Crapa

Sonoma, Napa, Mendocino, and Marin counties are a contiguous swath of prime Northern California real estate so beautiful that tourists can hardly wait to dump the ducats from their fanny packs. This, of course, comes with much provocation from the counties' respective tourism bureaus, which are not only doing their part to bring money into their counties but keep it from being siphoned by the neighboring counties. This is ironic since the areas they represent are practically related – the same family names are used for streets (the Fifths and the Bs are all fine folk), the same tribes of indigenous peoples were displaced, and the same earthquake is going to wipe us all out.

Until then, it's like the ultimate family feud. In wine country, sure, blood is thicker than wine, but cash is thicker than both because it's not a liquid. You could say, "We're all in it together." That is, we're all in a bare-knuckled brawl to win the hearts and travelers cheques of our visitors.

As Sonoma County's official "Lifestyle Ambassador" serving the Sonoma County Tourism Bureau, I am admittedly biased. I had a bidding war and Sonoma won, so I'm their man. To paraphrase the *Manchurian Candidate*, "Sonoma County is the kindest, bravest, warmest, most wonderful county I've ever known in my life." I'd say that even if they hadn't lined my pockets with dosh (as long as they showed me a queen of hearts.)

Sonoma is my native county – I was born in a granola patch in the west county hinterlands of Sebastopol. I've gotten as far as Sonoma Valley and might have kept going had I not broken my thumb in a hitchhiking accident. So defending Sonoma comes naturally to me. This is why I got a little edgy when some wag suggested that Napa consider stealing a page from the marketing plan of *Love Story* and spin "Love means never having to say you're sorry" into "Wine means never having to say you're Sonoma."

I can neither confirm nor deny this is true, in part because I haven't bothered trying. Why would I? Doing so would just risk empowering the slander by revealing its power to offend me. I've considered slogans to counter Napa's alleged campaign, like, "Napa is Crapa," which I realize is not only juvenile but likely to attract CRAPA, the Congleton Ramblers And Piss Artists (a UK walking group, "mostly from Congleton, who also like an odd pint or two" as their website explains – seriously, Google it) to ramble their way to Napa for a splash and slash. As its lifestyle ambassador, obviously, my official position is that I'd prefer to have a bunch of drunken Brits peeing all over *Sonoma* County. It's a wonderful place to pee, I do it all the time.

I suppose the only thing worse than having the English urinate in Napa instead of Sonoma would be to have them urinate in Marin. Thus we'd miss out on the, um, trickle-down effect that occurs between our wine countries. Marin doesn't really have a wine country, just a vineyard or two, probably purchased by a sucker who also owns pristine swampland in Florida. Instead of pretending to have a wine country, Marin should concentrate on building a hot tub time machine back to its 70s heyday. Marketing such a notion could be tricky – a slogan a la "Marin – You'll always come back – like herpes" somehow lacks the class of being greeted "Welcome back, Mrs. So-and-So" when checking into a Napa resort, even though you're not Mr. So-and-So's missus so much as his mistress.

Yes, I said it – Napa is where people go to cheat on their spouses. There's a reason most wineries are zoned such that weddings are prohibited – you can't have a wedding site that also trades in extramarital affairs – it violates anti-trust laws.

Also, it's only a matter of time before a James Bond-style supervillain builds a man-made island in international waters off the coast of California, declares it a nation, plants grapes on every square inch, and calls it "Wine Country." Then it would own worldwide rights on the term, effectively putting an end to Sonoma and Napa's dueling claim that each is the "real wine country. The rivalry between Napa and Sonoma will be moot anyway, however, when the next phylloxera plague destroys our mutual monoculture. The aphid's evil cousin, phylloxera take a particular delight in destroying vineyards, which unites our counties at least in fear.

That other grape-growing county, Mendocino, addresses this inevitability by diversifying its agriculture with marijuana. I mean, not officially, but come on, "The grass is greener in Mendocino" is more than a bumpersticker – it's an ad for a bumper crop of California gold. What do you think those red, white and green flags on all those trucks stand for? Zinfandel, Sauvignon Blanc and weed, man. Beware: Don't let anyone handle your baggage. The porters will swap it for ganja on your way out and suddenly you're trafficking illegal drugs between county lines – well, that was my defense anyway.

A more mature lifestyle ambassador might say the counties should work together to help tourists smoke dope and cheat on their spouses while steeping in a tub full of bubbly. But that guy isn't Sonoma's lifestyle ambassador – I am and I say, "If you didn't do it in Sonoma, you didn't do it at all."

The author in no way, shape, or form directly represents the interests of any of the aforementioned parties. He's just at a party – in his mind.

Zin Buddhism

Attention Sonoma "Buddhists." I think there's been some confusion between "zen" and "zin," which should be clarified post-haste lest someone attempt to achieve Nirvana – then wake up the next morning with a pounding headache.

As a spiritual-philosophical-neurological phenomenon, Enlightenment, categorically speaking, cannot be achieved with the contents of a bottle. Believe me, I've tried. No matter the vintage, no matter the grape, the results were always ever so-so. The wine is excellent, of course. It's the insights that go bust. False "profundancy" is best kept in the dorm room (between the hours of midnight and 3 a.m.) and first and last dates with so-called "spiritual" people who have not realized there's no such word and the term for which their wee minds are groping, in that long moment before you cry "check please," is "profoundness."

I believe the hiccup begins with trying to push the tenets of Eastern thought through a Western bottleneck. Buddhism: Desire is suffering. Sonoma: Hangovers are suffering. Sonoma reasoning: Ergo, hangovers are desirable.

Ultimately, wine might not be a means to achieve enlightenment so much as a way to help us endure those who claim to have achieved it themselves. This is how I've managed to keep such long friendships: I'm bloody brilliant and they're a bunch of drunks. Or perhaps it's the other way around. The point is, we need never know since the wine never ceases to flow. And when it does, at least one of us, the theory goes, will just jaunt down the eight-fold path to get some more.

It's been noted that a lot of writers torture the genius that tortures them with booze. Frankly, I think it's just an elaborate form of procrastination. Why else would we so frequently choose wine as our poison? Considering that it takes so damn long to open – what with peeling the foil, wrenching the reluctant cork after finding the eternally elusive corkscrew and then padding around one's hovel bemoaning the lack of clean glassware – one's muse has generally wandered off by the first sip. Then some wit toasts "To poetry!" Mercifully for him, everyone's too drunk to bother kicking his ass. This is called a writing group.

Poetry, of course, is where most attempts at spiritual observation coagulate like a black pudding of adolescent angst and marginalia from Huston Smith's "The World's Religions." So you took comparative religion in community college – do you have to write an epistolary poem about it?

You stars tonight are like fate's filament
A luminous light flickering, flame on wick
This beeswax candle just an instrument
In the bottle neck, with thumb upon a Bic

How *profundant*.

For some Sonomans, the cyclicality of life is most often experienced when peeing in a vineyard. You pee on the vines, the vines grow grapes, the grapes are made into wine, you drink the wine and then pee in the vineyard – balance achieved. That, however, is not achieving harmony with nature so much as treating our local agribusiness as a toilet. This is perhaps where Zin Buddhism likely exists, if it does at all: In nature or in a urinal. But then, a vineyard isn't really nature so much as it is an attempt to manage it. It's also not a urinal. Which is too bad in a way – the most profound observations are sometimes written on bathroom walls. Like the one that starts "There once was a man from Sonoma…" I can't remember how it goes but I know how it ends – Sunday morning worshipping the porcelain god, reckoning with being and nothingness.

Wine Country Weddings

So, you're finally getting hitched and one of you has the daft idea to have a wine country wedding. Chances are this bright idea arose because half of the couple thinks it's romantic and the other half foresees ready access to alcohol as a means to insure it will get done. You're both right, though more than a few vineyard workers might quibble about the romance part. But don't let that bother you, you're probably not inviting them anyway.

As someone who has both wed and remained married in wine country (these are mutually exclusive triumphs,) I know precisely what works, what doesn't, and how to prevent your wedding from becoming a reality TV show (though I do offer a "Prime Time Special" for those ready for their close-up). Yes, I am a wedding planner and I will spare you several thousand dollars in heartache and alimony if you pay close attention (and my nominal fee.)

In most places in the world, excessive wine-drinking ruins marriages. In Sonoma, it's what they're based on. In fact, not-drinking wine has led many a couple to the brink. Wine is the glue that binds us. It's worth noting that some translate "sommelier" as "marriage counselor." To wit, the notion of a "dry wedding" in Sonoma is more likely to evoke *extra brut* champagne than "alcohol free." In fact, the only "alcohol free" zone in Sonoma is likely the police department – at least during business hours. By the way, if the police show up at your wedding, chances are you are doing something either extremely wrong or extremely right, depending on the reddish hue of your neck.

Of course, the wine list is nearly as important as the guest list – in fact, more so, since one's memory is so easily imprinted by one's olfactory sense. Chances are you are more likely to recall a fine wine and its bouquet than some ancient relation. If, however, a relative's odor supercedes that of the wine, recommend them to a physician. And who invited them in the first place? Though there's no shame in being related to hobos, they are among the many reasons one might invest in a security guard. In Sonoma, where a general bonhomie permeates most activity (read: everyone is drunk), it's not uncommon to end up playing host to random strays. Weddings are particularly good targets for Sonoma's roving celebrators, who aren't opportunistic so much as merely confused (my own wedding was crashed by a certain city councilman, I kid you not.)

Any wedding planner will tell you: There's the pre-ceremony, ceremony, and reception; thereafter, however, most hardcore wedding-goers know there is also usually an after party, an after-after party and, as often, amateur stripping. Given the free flow of wine in Sonoma, there is the hazard of getting this sequence out of order. A good wedding planner will remain on site and make sure this doesn't happen, especially since bridal gowns are so difficult to get on in the first place and, unless green is one of your colors, the dollar bills stuffed in the décolletage might clash.

I advise inviting as many single guests as possible – it makes seating arrangements a breeze since aligning pair-bonded couples, who typically come in even numbers, invariably turns into some kind of people-Tetris. "So-

and-so can't be anywhere near such-and-such" because of some aborted romance, a failed business venture or other socially inconvenient back-story (see *The Graduate*) and suddenly you've got a human chess game. And, in the movies at least, human chess always leads to bloodshed.

Fortunately, dateless singletons are like social spackling. If there's a hole at a table because the work colleague you were obliged to invite "forgot" to bring their spouse you can simply patch it with a single-person, who will inherently be the most interesting person at the table. Why? Because they'll be the only person who won't have been bitching about the outlandish price of their accommodations in the hours preceding the ceremony – seasoned singles arrive without arrangements and with a sporting sense of where they might eventually lay. They also will not have driven the ungodly amount of hours it takes to get here from any place further than Napa, which, of course, is where they mistakenly arrived in the first place (take the left at Hwy. 12, "Sonoma / Boyes Hot Springs," not Highway 29 – trust me.)

If you are the token single-person at your table and want to hook up/need a place to crash, start early. That is, start drinking early. The sooner you get drunk the less it will matter where you wake up later. This is especially important since the Historic Sonoma Plaza, where many a singleton has rested a lonely head in the past, now runs its sprinkler system before dawn.

To that end, those interested in scoring with a woman at a wine country wedding should aim high and make a play for one of the bridesmaids. The fact is, they hate the ridiculous dresses forced onto them by the bride and can't wait to get out of them. This is where you can help. Likewise, for those who want to score with a man, aim low, specifically at the catering staff. Chances are, beneath those black and whites is a sensitive, sinewy, would-be artist with a simultaneous attraction and repulsion for those at whom he's been slinging crostini. This will easily heat into a "stable boy and lady of the manor" situation after he's thrown back a few unfinished bottles plucked from the bus tubs. Happens more than you will ever know.

Singletons, be assured that – no matter how discreet you are, how expertly you execute your dalliance like a clandestine CIA operation – everyone will know. And there will be photos. And they will be on Facebook. Who, you ask, would deign to behave so cheaply? The bride and groom. At around the third day of their "wine country honeymoon," the dull decadence of wineries and room service loses its charm and life's rhythms of quiet disappointment and abject tedium resume. To allay these feelings, many newlyweds default to gossiping about their wedding guests, which inevitably leads to the echo-chamber of social media. Especially when there's photographic evidence. Bonus points for video. Add a splash of one of Sonoma's fine vintages, a smidge of buyer's remorse and the "catty" gets let out the bag quite quickly. You'll wish said bag was on your head – or that of your new friend.

The only way to rectify the situation, mitigate the shame and recast the entire episode as a romantic turn of fate is to marry that person. I know it sounds rash, but chances are you already got the rash. To wit, I offer an array of wine country wedding planning services to help you avoid, as one of my colleagues put it, "The 'whine' in wine and the 'count' in 'country.'" Mazel tov.

Time Travelin' Man

In my line of work, I'm often required to be a bit of a time traveler. You see, the subject of today's message is Fall, which won't have officially transpired until after I've filed these precious words (the Autumnal Equinox is Sept. 21). However, I must also write as if it's already happened since these words won't be released to the public until the Friday after. So, I'm writing for the future as if it's already the past. It begs the question, is Fall falling or fallen at this point? This is the kind of query best suited for Lewis Carroll and H.G. Wells to hash out over absinthe. If those fellows ever invited me, sure, I'd join them but it wouldn't help the fact that both me and Fall are past deadline.

To look outside in Northern California, you'd think it was Spring, but Spring on Venus, you know, where the planet's proximity to the sun causes temperatures to be in excess of 770 degrees Fahrenheit. You Sonomans complaining about the heat on Facebook should be grateful to be one rock further from the sun. Why is it that our once bracing autumnal weather feels like someone left the door open to Hell? Let's turn to history.

Shortly after Al Gore invented the Internet, the presidency was stolen from him. As his utopian vision of a world interconnected by the Information Superhighway crumbled, he became morose, grew a beard and created a weather machine to crank the heat on a world that had forsaken him. That's what the plot of *An Inconvenient Truth* was, right? I don't know, I couldn't get past the first 15 minutes. Regardless, it's nearly October and the mercury is still rising. At this rate, come November, our Thanksgiving turkeys will cook themselves. We might crawl into the oven ourselves, as it will likely be cooler than it is outside.

Mother Nature is probably just stoned. Any moment, she'll come to, rub her eyes, and get on with adding a little chill to the wind and some dashes of orange and burnt umber to the trees. If she doesn't wake up, if she's in a coma, say, or worse – dead – it would make a terrific third act for Al Gore to come back and redeem his evil ways by reviving her with some other technological whiz-bang. At least then he'd have something to put on Current TV.

Of course, Al Gore isn't really the Lex Luthor of climate change. He's the Jimmy Olsen – well-meaning, but kind of worthless without Superman. Whomever Eco-Superman turns out to be, I know it won't be me. I'm the kind of cad who gleefully climbs into my car on "Spare the Air" days to take advantage of the lack of traffic. So, I suppose, in point of fact, it's people like me we can blame for our forestalled Fall.

Like the columns I write for the future-past, perhaps I should pen an apology to future generations for messing up the climate. Yeah, I'll take that one on personally since no one else seems willing. And no, I'm not subsidized by Big Oil or any other gross polluters to be their official scapegoat. I'm just a guy who remembers crisp air, crunching leaves and a haze on the horizon around this time a year. I should probably also write up a description of what Fall used to be like in Northern California, where it might just find its most beautiful annual expression, so the children of tomorrow can appreciate what a villain I was. Then they'll invent a time machine to travel back in time to kick my ass and discover they're outnumbered.

Liquid Assets

In the world of wine marketing, there's something for everybody. Consider the two press releases I received this morning, within minutes of each other. One came from Ashley Systma at People's Wine Market and the other from Anna Miller of 42 West. As one might infer from their respective names, each represents a decidedly different place on the economic spectrum.

Put "People's" in front of any noun (I'm thinking "People's Park" or "People's Revolution" of insert-country-name-here) and we know implicitly there's no money in it. Because the people are broke. If they weren't broke they'd have a better name, like "Ruling Class." That's at least what came to mind when I read Systma's PR, which was headlined "Artisan Wineries Sit on Stockpile of Recession-Era Vintages." Throughout, Systma posits a David and Goliath relationship between the artisan wineries and their "corporate competition," which has been amplified by the slow economic recovery. Systma's new website promises to turn overstock into a "marketing asset and provide customers with deals" because "as a new vintage became available, older vintages were pushed aside." Alas, a "wine glut;" a term that, heretofore, I've only used to describe my abdominal woes.

The upshot, I suppose, is to raise a raise a glass of discounted wine and say "Power to the people!" Just don't do it near Christie's at Rockefeller Center in New York next week, lest an auctioneer think you're bidding on a rare Inglenook wine from Francis Ford Coppola's private collection. Dubbed the "Rebirth of a Legend" by the fine folks at 42 West, I cannot help but think the wines on offer, particularly two bottles of the "legendary 1941 Inglenook," are little more than the spoils of a highfalutin' garage sale. Perhaps this writer (and, by extension, his esteemed readership) isn't the target market for 70-year-old wines. Apparently Coppola isn't either since he's finally dumping them – they've been in his cellar since he purchased the former Inglenook estate back in 1975, when I was first developing my love of the bottle, albeit one full of milk.

So why now, Francis? The upcoming auction is codenamed "Renaissance," though I think "Liquid Assets" would've been more apt. For that matter, why does a wine auction need a codename anyway? Especially a codename cited in a press release. Good thing 42 West wasn't running intelligence in WWII, otherwise we'd all be speaking German.

"A truly unique offering is a bottle so rare that the estate would only part with one: the 1935 vintage from the 'Golden Era...'" Pray tell, what does a Golden Era bottle of wine run? About $600. Pricey for vinegar but much less than I expected given the breathless hyperbole of the press release. I mean, I've had phone bills bigger than that. For $600 you can get round trip airfare to NYC, never get off the plane and still drink better wine, if you know what I'm saying. Of course, that little single-serve, screw-capped bottle won't come with a handwritten note from Coppola in a custom-made wooden box as promised by the press release. But you could probably get a flight attendant to sign your cocktail napkin with a little hustle. Unless there's some TSA rule against it and they have to land the plane because you're brandishing a Sharpie.

Suffice it to say, if that happens to you, I'll personally buy you a bottle of Coppola's wine from PeoplesWineMarket. com and we'll cue up *Apocalypse Now* on Netflix and write our own wine press release with the headline "This is the End, My Only Friend, the End."

Wired Wine

Each month, *Wired* magazine features a front-of-book item entitled "What's Inside," in which they break down the chemical components that make up various products. In the current issue, it's red wine.

Some of the ingredients were to be expected (ethanol, tannins,) though some sounded like erstwhile CIA psychedelic experiments (malvidin 3-glucoside, tyramine, 2-methoxy-pyrazine.) Though these chemcials are all naturally occurring, would anyone really notice if someone slipped in a little somethin'-somethin' from the MK-Ultra program? Yes, but they wouldn't be able to talk about it until the next morning when the flowers stopped singing to them.

What *Wired* failed to list in its breakdown of our beloved beverage were what we might call the alchemical ingredients of wine – the magic, the passion, the love, the corpse buried in the vineyard. Yes, "terror and terroir" gags aside, you and I both know there is a statistical probability of a body being deep-sixed in someone's vineyard somewhere.

After 150 years in the wine biz, Sonoma has certainly seen its share of homicides, so it's not really that difficult to imagine that the fertile soils of our wine country have been turned by at least one wayward shovel. Think about all the dynastic struggles, the obvious motives, and ready access to vineyards (leave the Plaza in any direction and you'll hit one within half a mile.) Yep, that dark note you can't put your finger on in the tasting room could very likely be a little dash of death. Yum.

This is not a unique thought — plenty of jerk-offs before me have mulled the notion, with or without criminal intent. However, I say it's high time for *CSI: Sonoma* to get its butt in gear and get out here with a couple of bloodhounds and maybe even a psychic with a divining rod for the dead. One set of skeletal human remains and we can get a lock on the emerging goth market. Our local sommeliers could start asking if one "cares for a little film noir with your pinot noir?" The term "Sonomacide" will become a staple of true-crime books and the band name of alt-rock darlings *Death Cab for Cutie* will finally make some sense.

Of course, learning the extent to which one's mourvedre is macabre might prove lethal to the wine industry as much as the poor schmuck whose flesh is its fertilizer. Perhaps we should concentrate on other secret ingredients – like pee.

Don't act so surprised. One out of five Sonomans have peed in a vineyard – most out of necessity, some out of sport. I can't tell you how many times I've heard a triumphal recollection of some gang's "crazy night" that featured urinating outdoors in a vineyard. Oddly, it's mostly been women. Sure, dudes like to pee outside to affirm the fact that they can with the wildest of ease. A dude would pee in the wind and expect an answer if Bob Dylan told him so. However, it's the ladies, usually after hitting a few tasting rooms as a bridal send-off, who are most apt to scamper off and rain rivulets of used wine into Sonoma soil. There are several possible reasons for this, which range from the biological to the sociological with a lot of drunkeness in between. Suffice it to say, if descriptors like "cadaver" and "urinal" creep into our tasting notes, remember, you heard it here first.

Locovores vs. Cannibals

A few years ago, the *Oxford American Dictionary*'s dons of definition welcomed the term "locavore" into its hallowed pages. As you may recall, the term refers to those that graze on grub grown within a 100 mile radius of where they live. Where some might call this lazy or xenophobic, others find it an environmentally-conscious pursuit that adds *Sesame Street*-level game play to one's grocery shopping. Neeeear... Farrr...

Of course, in Wine Country, our local bounty is such that locavorism is second nature. Or technically, just nature since we've got it all and wine to boot. In fact, an extreme locavore might suggest our wine is all you need to survive. And for a while, they'd be right – until their system shuts down because their blood alcohol level is more the latter than the former. Though I admire the local spirit, I can't stand the term locavore, which is simply one of the ugliest words to be admitted into the English language. Even "crepuscular," which sounds like a crepe that works out, is more attractive than locavore. Locavore sounds like a locomotive living la vida loca. Basically, it's a ride on the "crazy train" and it's bringing in the holidays. Local turkey – check; local veggies – check; local "I can't believe your trampy sister brought that three-time loser she's dating to Thanksgiving dinner" – check, check, check.

Yep, it's a locacopia. Of course one might assume we'd have coined our own version of locavorism by now. But somehow "Sonomavore" isn't as catchy, unless you think of it as "She gave him Sonomavores. And now his wife has them too."

Sonomans are omnivores anyway and more inclined to eat a locavore than be one. Following on the maxim, "You are what you eat," however, Sonomans are locavores by default. Not to mention cannibals. Hence our local adage, "Chew me once, shame on you; chew me twice, shame on me. Now I'm leftovers."

But what if you're a Vegetarian-American, you ask? If the annually rising sales of Tofurkeys are any indication, there's a chance you'll either have a vegetarian at your Thanksgiving table or you are one. Good for you but any notion of being a locavore is DOA (that's carnivore slang for "well done"). You see, Tofurkys are not native to this planet. Or any planet. Tofurkys are to birds what cyborgs are to humans – about half-right, half-wrong with a whole lotta technology in between. In the strictest sense, they're beans that have been processed into the shape of a football, though not as edible. It's been conjectured that they were a 1950s monster movie prop that escaped and bred in the wild.

All I know is that I once knew a dude who bragged that he "never ate anything with a face on it," so I stuck googly eyes on his Tofurky and watched the psychic fallout from across the room. I couldn't tell if he was choked up or just choking but the waterworks ran for about half an hour. This is among the many holiday memories I'll cherish forever.

Yes, I'm a holiday bully, which I blame entirely on my annual (over-)consumption of local wine. My name is Daedalus Howell and I'm a "winovore." As you let the genius of this neologism set in, permit me to extol the virtues of its central premise – drink only wine grown and vinted in our area. It's good for the local economy and it's a great fall-back position when someone has the gall to ask "What are you thankful for this Thanksgiving?"

You need only take a sip, nod and say "I'm thankful for the opportunity to support the local agriculture and economy of our fair burg. And it pairs so well with the Tofurky, don't you think?"

Night Train

Though Sonoma County won't be getting its high-speed rail anytime soon, we once again have freight trains rumbling through the valley. An article in the local rag reads "Northwestern Pacific Railroad moved a three-car train from Lombard Junction in Napa County" and "the train moved through the sloughs before crossing the Wingo Bridge."

First off, shouldn't that be "Wino Bridge?" and secondly, Wingo has a bridge? Didn't we just show them the secret of fire and the wheel? They're advancing rather quickly – it's only a matter of time before the Wingonads try to overthrow their Sonoma oppressors, you know, with sticks and stones and the indomitable spirit of the underdog. Like in the movies. We're doomed. That is, unless they try to ride the train into town, in which case they'll just end up in Petaluma – where they belong.

Of course none of this can compete, at least in Napa's collective mind, with their so-called Wine Train. Rumor has it that back in the day, a band of rogue Sonomans attempted a "robbery" of the wine train astride horses in a manner reminiscent of "The Great Train Robbery" (which, scholars of cinema will remember, is the first film to depict locomotive larceny.) Though I doubt Napa will reciprocate with a reprisal upon our three-car little-engine-that-could, I do anticipate a sudden spike in hobo traffic to Sonoma from Napa and beyond. Trains, and the hopping of them, have long been the hobo's preferred mode of travel. I'm surprised Amtrak never considered creating a Hobo Express to exploit the market. They could serve Night Train and Mulligan Stew on the dining car. Napa wouldn't know what hit them.

I've not hopped the rails myself but my kid brother experienced some rail-borne adventures in his late teens with a drifter named "Squinty." It's no wonder he took to the road so well when he later became a rock star and lived much of the aughts aboard a tour bus. Like rock stars, hobos are just carnies with ADD, meaning they can't stay in one place too long for fear of boredom and paternity suits. This probably accounts for all the amount of train songs in rock 'n' roll (or at least the one, "Train Kept a Rollin'" that everyone covers.) There's even a band called Train, which, incidentally, no one covers.

With Sonoma's new found train-awareness, perhaps we could start using that catchy Brit phrase "mind the gap," the recorded advisory that reminds tube passengers of the precarious space between the train and its platform. Of course, it will only take 15 minutes before some wine marketer starts using it as slogan for the so-called Petaluma Gap appellation (though the proposed designation sounds more like an outlet mall than it does a contender for an American Viticultural Area). Likewise, Depot Park Museum might see a spike in traffic, if not from hobos then from other travelers interested in our own reliquary of rail. With all this train on the brain, it comes as no surprise that the Sonoma Valley Wine Trolley rolls into town Friday after next, boasting several winery stops and a lunch catered by the Girl and the Fig (no Night Train since the Fig only serves Rhone varietals).

Fair warning to those with a romantic yen to illegally ride the rails: it's a brilliant way to lose a limb. According to the Federal Railroad Administration, in 2010, there were 2,837 grade crossing and railroad trespassing accidents in the US, resulting in 712 fatalities and 1,192 serious injuries, which accounts for the trendy hobo name "Stumpy."

I'm not sure what fuels trains these days (besides nostalgia) but I do know there could be worse chugging across the valley – a horde of velociraptors, for example, or Sonoma music columnist James Marshall Berry on a unicycle. With a heave, and a ho, I just couldn't tell him so... All aboard!

Daedalus Howell Wrote Here

In my travels of late, I've noticed a tourism trend Sonoma has yet to cultivate. It's requires a bit of a grave-robbing and possibly some plagiarism but nothing any self-respecting visitors bureau wouldn't hesitate doing for its local economy. At least a couple comparably-sized cities have made mints by claiming affinities with dead European authors with whom they have little Earthly connection. Sonoma could do the same with its own mascot wordsmith, from whence will come heads in beds and keepsakes in the carry-ons from everything from highbrow festivals (read: it's expensive to feel classy) to wretched, ink-stained bobbleheads (it's also pricey to feel trashy.)

Consider Ashland, OR, home of the annual theatrical juggernaut the Oregon Shakespeare Festival, which has minted millions since its founding in 1935 – predicated on boosting the Bard, centuries after his death and 5,121 miles by air from his place of residence. Relationship to Ashland prior to the advent of the festival? None whatsoever. But since the planning commission mandated a style guide straight from the Renaissance Faire, the place has a distinctly Elizabethan air. Or as the local businesses call it, "Ka-ching."

Solvang, the so-called Danish capital of America, is nestled in Santa Barbara County wine country which, like our wine country, will be kaput in 30 years due to climate change, according to a recent Stanford University study.

(Special thanks to colleague Ashlie Rodiguez of the *L.A. Times* who wrote about the issue and kindly forwarded her source material.) Apart from its allegiance to Hamlet's habitue and decor that could only be called mid-millennia modern, Solvang seems to have little else going for it. That is until one considers its adoption of Denmark's greatest author export Han Christian Andersen (yeah, I thought it was Søren Kierkegaard too.) The town's local bookstore boasts a museum dedicated to the teller of tales that includes a bust so fascinating in its grotesque depiction of Andersen that one becomes hypnotized and invariably leaves with a few books under one's arm.

Of course, Glen Ellen has long laid claim to action-adventure penman Jack London. Could they do more with their literary legacy? Sure, you know, after the California state budget crisis runs its course (into the apocalypse.) As author Timothy Egan opined at NYTimes.com, "Jack London State Historic Park will be shuttered, gates locked, and left to meth labs, garbage outlaws, and assorted feral predators." 'Nuff said..

So, which literary lion will purr for the tourists in Sonoma? I'm not dead yet so I'm out of the running (though I have considered faking my death so that we could enjoy my posthumousness together – you know, at the foot of my life-sized statue in the Plaza.) Whomever the candidate, the model heretofore, seems to favor the canon, meaning dead European males (Go figure – it was other dead European males who made the cannon.) Also, they should have some international name recognition to attract pilgrimages by the jet-load but be obscure enough not to have already been claimed by another city (see above.)

My research (five minutes ago on Wikipedia) led me to at least one possibility. No drum roll, please – no one's heard of this guy for the better part of a century. But he's got some street cred in 19th century Paris, plays to revive, and a grudge against sobriety, which we could position as an abiding love of wine. Consider **Alfred Jarry. Who?** The proto-surrealist was something like the Lenny Bruce of his day but without all the censorship hoo-haw (and a lot more TB.) His most famous and now forgotten work, the play *Ubu Roi*, opened with a the single word "Merdre" which, pardon my French, roughly translates as "crap-esque." Yep, it's prime for a wine country revival. Also, I bear a passing resemblance to him so, when the time comes, you'll only have to change the plaque on the statue.

Your Questions Answered, Sonoma

Given the deluge of mail I receive in my professional capacity as Sonoma's scribe du jour – be it actual, virtual, or otherwise – I'm frequently at a loss as to how to answer it all and still make my weekly deadline. After years on this beat (technically I'm the in-house bon vivant, though no one confirms nor denies this to my face), it finally occurred to me that I could make my deadline and reply to my correspondance by simply doing it here, on the paper's dime.

Clearly, I'm a genius. Why Sonoma Valley High School has yet to grant me an honorary diploma is beyond comprehension (which I spelled all by myself without spell-check, by the way – or "btw" as we of sophomore-level educations might say). Nvrthls, I'm going to attempt to kill two birds with one stone, or at least get two birds stoned as Brit rocker Ian Billings might say. Ahem.

Dear Daedalus:
Is "Daedalus Howell" your real name or did you steal it from a brand of Greek dog food? – Sleepless in Sonoma

Dear Sleepless – (If that is indeed *your* real name) "Daedalus Howell" is my legal name but not my original name. That was Alpolis Purinas, which actually is Greek for "dog food" and a painful nightmare from which I thought I'd awoken. Apparently, not – so, yeah, thanks for bringing it up.

Dear DH: How did you end up in Sonoma? – Curious N. Curiouser

Curious you should ask (couldn't resist). Like many who "end up" in Sonoma, I got lost on the way to Napa. Also, my palm reader says I'm cursed. (But what does it know? It's just an iPhone app.) And I fell in love. (Sigh.) Then I got over myself and realized that if I was ever going to make it as a small-time media mogul I'd have to start small and stay small. I immediately recognized the limited opportunities and resources surrounding me and knew that I was home – or, at any rate, I wasn't going anywhere anytime soon and had to make the least of it. The rest, as they say, is mystery.

Dear Sir: I am a diplomatic attache and in-law to the late President, General Sanni Abacha of Nigeria. Amata, his first born son is facing difficulty obtaining his inheritance and I seek your assistance us in securing some funds, abroad for safe keeping. We are willing to offer you 15% of the funds after the transaction for your co-operation. All I need from you is an assurance in the form of a small deposit of several thousand dollar. Be rest assured that there is no risk involved since I have taken care of everything. Awaiting with interest. Sincerely, Farouk Bakoh.

Farouk – Dude, I'm in. You had me at "Nigeria." I've got several similar deals going with Nigerian diplomats and am totally stoked to have another. Man, I tell ya, when these babies pay off, I might just buy Nigeria a big fat present to say "Thanks!" How 'bout a little piece of wine country we call "Glen Ellen?" Yours. Done. Okay, so where do I send the check? Do you take PayPal? Let's do this. Thanks for thinking of me (sorry it took so long to reply!) – DH

Rain Pain

It finally stopped raining. Strip off your clothes, soak in some vitamin D and mourn the loss of the 2011 vintage. Blame it on climate change or Al Gore or a wrathful God trying to wash away the last of those odious "Rapture" billboards. The point is, the unseasonal deluge is not only record-breaking but potentially heartbreaking for many in our wine industry. Fortunately, I was able to call in a favor with a certain Bond villain I know and got us a little sunshine this weekend. You're welcome, Sonoma.

For some grape growers, it could be too late. The damage is done. It's as if Spring and all that the season entails in terms of pollination and fertility amongst the vines was washed away with a bucket of cold water thrown by a schoolmarm upon necking teenagers. The wetter weather has made fertilization in the vineyard a non-starter with soggy pollen spores unable to make their destinations. Here's some "birds and bees" notes I cribbed online:

Following bloom, part of the flower called a "cap" separates and exposes the "anthers," which in turn release their pollen. Pollen flies around and eventually lands on the stigma and pistil of other flowers resulting in pollination wherein multiple pollen grains germinate, creating a pollen tube into the pistil, then to the ovary and finally the ovule where a sperm and egg form an embryo (that last part should sound familiar.) Rain screws up this process as it would, pretty much, for any creatures swapping DNA unless they're in a romantic movie.

Here's another possible problem: If the rains continue deeper into summer, the grapes that do arrive might end up resembling water balloons. Vineyard managers frequently "stress" their grapes by reducing their water intake to a trickle to encourage complexity. By that token, ours might become the least-stressed grapes ever grown – they'll be like stoners lined on the beach of an island resort, passing a joint and wondering if "mellow" and "marshmallow" share an etymological root, man.

Our grapes could get so plump with liquid that the notion of becoming, say, a raisin was washed away weeks ago. Not that many wine grapes aspire to be raisins, but those that did have forever lost that opportunity and "opportunity is what makes this country grape," one might imagine their leader saying in a stump speech.

Speaking of stumps, whole vineyards could be mowed to their root stock, making way for strip malls and box stores, if we don't start buying local wine by the case and keep our producers in business (hey, it beats hosting a charity car wash – especially when it's raining.)

We should also consider altering our local topography to reduce the impact of future storms. Obviously, Sonoma Mountain needs to be higher since it can't currently produce a "rain shadow." This is what results when mountains cast a "shadow" of dryness on their leeward side by blocking the weather. As a hack, of course, I'm more taken with the pseudo-poetry of "Rain Shadow" than its actual meaning. It sounds like a cheap cologne I might have worn in the 80s. Splash on some Rain Shadow and suddenly you smell of wet wool and cigarettes and are prone to linger outside shop windows always waiting for Her and muttering "Compulsion" in a British accent.

If the rain continues through Fall, we may have to harvest our grapes like they do cranberries – their beds are flooded and the floating fruit is pumped into vats. Don't be alarmed if you see vineyard workers in scuba gear and butterfly nets come harvest. Unless, of course, it's canceled. Unfortunately, the wine industry can't pay its bills with rain-checks.

Sonomaste

Yoga and wine – there is always someone trying to put these two wildly disparate concepts together. The reasons span commerce to comedy, though the latter is usually unintentional. Many of these daring souls are friends of mine; others are the criminally insane. Some are both. Please consider these words confirmation that wine and yoga do not "pair" as it were. In fact, it's downright dangerous. I'll explain.

New Year's Eve, 2006 – my then band and I were ending the worst gig we ever played. Three songs into the set. Our patron, sommelier to the stars Christopher Sawyer, had a rare lapse in his finesse at creating harmony by coupling this and that when he booked our rock act with the traditionally staid audience of a prix fixe dessert experience at the Lodge at Sonoma. Suffice it to say, when it became apparent that the frequencies of our amps was curdling the cream in the eclairs (let alone the batteries in the hearing aids of those for whom we were performing), Sawyer diplomatically suggested we sit out the set with a complimentary bottle of bubbly.

Somewhere along the line, my then girlfriend (now wife, the Contessa) arrived at my Springs studio, whereupon someone lost a bet (me) that resulted in an impromptu yoga session from the Contessa. There was apparently some question as to whether or not I could perform "bakasana," which I've since learned is not a Middle Eastern menu item but rather Sanskrit for "crow pose." Simply put, you willfully defy the laws of physics and lift your body from the mat with your palms down while levitating your knees behind your upper arms. Then you eat crow. Well, that's the polite way of putting it. Ether way, you eat it. Or at least your nose does, especially when you've been partying with Sawyer. Our crow pose ended with couple of bruised beaks.

Now, mind you, I have nothing against wine or yoga. The Contessa herself is a certified yoga instructor (naturally, she was certified post-crow incident). Moreover, I bear no grudge for wine. I've drained oceans of it. I'm personally responsible for the Great Sonoma Wine Drought of '08. That said, the crook in my nose tells me that wine and yoga do not a meritage make. It's more like "triage."

Now, you say, "DH, no one advocates drinking wine while practicing yoga." True, but that hasn't prevented a few daft would-be yogis from trying. Every half an hour I receive a press release from someone touting some kind of "wine country meets yoga" gig. Even Karl Wente, the fifth generation winemaker in Livermore and "devoted yoga practitioner" has released his own yoga videos in which he shares "how yoga has encouraged balance and focus in his life, allowing him to become acutely in-tune with the wines he creates..."

I've partied with the dude while on assignment and one way I achieved balance in his midst was by alternating between the wine bar and the kegerator in the basement. Albeit, this is more "um" than "om" but upon receiving the release, I immediately conflated Wente's two separate pursuits in my addled mind because of the persistent threat I perceive of them uniting somewhere in Sonoma.

I mentioned this to a tasting room manager who sardonically replied, "Wine and yoga – that's a stretch" as she pulled on a puffer vest, obscuring the Lululemon logo on the back of her shirt. From Sanskrit "Namaste" translates to "the spirit in me respects the spirit in you." In Sonoma, it just might mean "conspiracy theory."

This Bud's for You

Back before everyone got all fancy-like, "bud break" in Sonoma meant something other than the annual protrusion of leafy blossoms in our vineyards. Bud breaks were once as ubiquitous as the proverbial coffee break (this was, of course, before anyone could afford real beer, so Budweiser had to suffice).

Now, few wine regions can stand up to the excellence of our yearly yield. This is why it infuriates me when I overhear some lumpen, fanny-packing tourist adulating over the beauty of our "wine fields." Albeit, I should be grateful that these kind people have traveled from hither and yon to pour their good money into our local economy. But this errant wine-through-fields notion (or "WTF" as the kids might say) lends to the impression that bottles of wine grow on trees and as convenient as that would be, it overlooks the contribution of dozens of people who've dedicated their lives to making wine – namely our winemakers.

Perhaps this is karmic fallout from the legion of publicists who, all at once it seemed, decided to start referring to the wineries and winemakers that retained them as "farms" and "farmers."

Quaint as this is (and often true, though not always), it's led to the understandable if asinine collapsing of the concepts of a vineyard and a field of, say, wheat or whatever it is they're growing out there in the American heartland, in the minds of our visitors.

Of the two crops for which California is famous, one is so special that the place where it originates is accorded a unique name (and, no, it's not "hydroponics"). Hence, we say "vineyards" instead of "field of grapes." Only grapes are grown in vineyards. Nothing else. If they could make wine from soybeans (and trust me, Monsanto is surely working on it), they will eventually think of a classy-sounding name for soybean fields. Like "tofurchards." Until this inevitable "beanery with scenery" situation arises, we must acknowledge the work of our various vineyard personnel and insist that their territory of toil be called what they are – vineyards.

Some credit the ancient peoples of what is now the sovereign state of Georgia (the one south of Russia, not where the peach schnapps fields are) for first creating wine around 8,000 B.C. News traveled fast back then, at least geologically speaking, so about 3,000 years later, the Greeks either finally got the memo or discovered the magic powers of fermented grapes on their own. It's not hard to imagine some toga-wearing average Iosif witnessing an animal noshing on some naturally fermented berries and merrily staggering away.

Yes, we learned about booze from animals, and to celebrate the discovery we act like them when we're drunk.

Anyway, the Roman Empire knocked viticultural production up a few notches by bringing slaves into the vineyards. In 4 A.D., a chap named Gaius penned *Lex Aelia Sentia*, a student law primer that explained, among other things, how slaves could achieve Roman citizenship through their vineyard labors. Curiously, when the slaves became citizens they didn't care to work in the vineyards any longer and Roman winemaking flagged. Fast-forward a few dozen centuries as the Europeans continued to refine winemaking techniques until, finally, they were perfected circa 2005 here in Sonoma (this also happens to be the year I arrived – coincidence?)

Given the millennia people have devoted their lives to cultivating grapes for sake of making wine, the least we could do is honor their labor by using the correct terminology. Someday, perhaps a misguided turista will look up from his visitor's guide and having failed to find "wine field" in the index, instead chance upon another word and form labiodental fricative necessary to finally say "vineyard." When that day comes, he will proclaim "This bud break is for you."

Through a Wine Glass, Darkly

Readers often ask, "Where do you get your ideas?" After I swallow the bile that wells up in my esophagus (nothing personal – just a Pavlovian response I developed while slumming on the workshop circuit) I tell my fellow Sonomans to "look in the mirror." When, indignant, they ask, "What the hell does that mean, man?" I patiently explain, "YOU are my inspiration."

If this is followed by awkward blushing and "ah, shucks" shoe-gazing, I clarify by adding that I mean "you" in the general, colloquial sense, a la "the collective consciousness of Sonoma." At least when there is consciousness and we're not all face down in the Plaza clutching 750s of Gloria Ferrer. This is followed by understanding or disappointment – sometimes both – then their brow furrows as if they're asking themselves, "Wait, should I be offended?"

As patronizing as the preceding paragraphs may read, it's true – much of my Sonoma-themed work comes from direct experience with Sonomans. And sometimes the police.

While at the cafe this week, Chief Sackett strolled up to jovially suggest that I might someday consider getting a real office. I reminded him that it's from such establishments that I glean my material. Then I lamented, "It's not as easy as writing the police blotter, you know," which, he agreed, sort of "writes itself." The DUI arrests alone could fill our bi-weekly news-hole but since our editor is an environmentalist, he'd rather spare the trees and just run the more ludicrous ones.

If I ribbed Chief Sackett that in the "social satire trade," blotter fodder are low-hanging fruit he might remind me that the blotter is actual reportage, not shtick. Then, my tenuous faith in humanity would be devastated. Indeed, observational humor shouldn't require a breathalyzer – unless it's the punch line to a "You know you're a Sonoman when…" kind of gag.

And if I ever devolve into that sort of nit-wittery please buy my soul back for me – I'll owe you. It'll be cheap, trust me – probably less than my wee fee for writing this crap in the first place. Hey, I don't mind being a hack but hackneyed is something else entirely. I bet.

Besides, to "know you're a Sonoman when…" is ontologically impossible in my opinion. As any two-glass guru will tell you, the state of Sonomanhood is more an act of becoming than being. On top of that, it brings up the sticky question of defining what a Sonoman IS. The list of what a Sonoman is not, of course is infinite but I can assure you that topping it are "sober," "Napan" and "sober."

Then there are Sonoma-specific experiences like WitchiePoo and Glarifees and getting a bear hug from J.M. Berry that lasts just a little too long. Sure, it sounds like "Alice and Wonderland" on a bad date but it's our bad date, damn it. Just remember one pinot makes you larger and one pinot makes you small. And tonight we've got a sitter and $20 with "Vern's Taxi" written all over it.

I used to think of life in Sonoma as a long, hard look

into a funhouse mirror – a kind of comic distortion through a wine glass, darkly. It magnifies eccentricities into virtues and skews perspective along a vineyard-lined horizon where a rosy sun is always setting. Now, I realize it's more akin to a leap through the looking glass, with preconceptions snapping underfoot like so many shards. Just as you can't see your own face without a mirror, there comes a point when you can't see Sonoma any longer because you've become it. Then you have to search its shadows in the eyes of others. And that's where I get my ideas.

Snake in the Glass

Spring is a time of renewal, when even the snakes lying in the grass of our local Eden shed their skins and slither about their business with a little more rattle in their prattle.

I'm all for change but it was jarring when I expected to see the tawny awning that usually skirts the Sonoma Hotel and adjacent brasserie the Girl and the Fig, and instead spied the skeletal frame beneath it. Of course, I understand it's temporary but it looks as if an erector set has been grafted onto the side of the building a la the ducts and whatnot adorning the Centre Georges Pompidou in Paris.

Mind you, I'm a fan of modern architecture, even in the precious 4th arrondissement, however, seeing the building of my one of my usual joints essentially naked was disconcerting. I had to drink twice as many pintos to get my eyes to adjust, which brings me to the utter revulsion I experienced when I read of the proposal to pave up to 75% of the Historic Sonoma Plaza for additional street parking. I can drink an ocean of pintos and guarantee my eyes will never adjust to the sight of cars pulling into spaces where our picnic tables once were.

Though the proposed "Re-allocation of Historic Sonoma Plaza Spatial Resources" spares the two children's playgrounds, I can hardly imagine any parent would want their child playing anywhere near an operating parking lot.

That the plan includes a "valet station/babysitting post" is little consolation. Parking cars and sitting kids are two entirely different activities, how City Hall thinks that a single employee could handle both positions simultaneously is beyond comprehension. Yes, I agree "creating jobs" and "providing childcare" are noble pursuits but not all at once, in one person. Who even has that kind of resume besides, like, actors?

Also, I think that the premise of a drive-thru wine tasting gazebo is utterly absurd if not illegal. We already have a drunk-driving epidemic in town -- do we need to encourage it with the so-called "Splash-n-Dash?" Besides, if you're parked on the Plaza (let alone in the Plaza) chances are you're already drunk. I mean, "one for the road" is bad enough – "one ON the road" is downright reprehensible.

Likewise, "compensating for the relative loss of recreational space with the inclusion of a merry-go-round in the proposed traffic circle" hardly makes up for the devastation to the trees, lawns and, not to mention, hard-won history that constitutes our beloved Plaza. How does one even get to the merry-go-round when a legion of cars is constantly circling it? I suppose that's what the inane "recommendation to the Sonoma Unified School District for a required course in crossing guardianship" is meant to address. First off, what does that even mean? City Hall is going to make it mandatory for Sonoma children to be crossing guards, so other kids can get to a carnival ride in the middle of a drunk driving derby? If this isn't a prescription for disaster I don't know what is except for the proposal to turn the duck pond into a car wash by adding towels. Has City Hall ever seen the water in that pond? Or, rather, is that water in the pond? And how is the duck pond car wash going to be staffed? By requiring a class called "Towel?" This is insanity, people.

Let's just hope that the parties responsible for this insult grow a little backbone before it comes up for review April 1 and cancel this premises without compromise. As Harriet Tubman advised "Never wound a snake; kill it."

Grape Press

As Sonoma County's lifestyle ambassador, it is occasionally my duty (nay, pleasure!) to escort members of the international press through our fair burg. My most recent excursion with foreign media was last Saturday, when I accompanied Andre Domaine of Germany's *Weinwelt* magazine through a few wine tastings (Buena Vista, Bart Park, and B.R. Cohn all showed well) and a luncheon at the Girl and the Fig (Domaine was so taken, he ran out of German words whilst singing its praises, so I loaned him some English words.) What will eventually appear in *Weinwelt* is anyone's guess, not least of which because it will be in another language.

This much I know – Google translates Domaine's magazine name as "Wine World," though its German pronunciation sounds exactly like one's English after parading through a few tasting rooms – especially if you mispronounce the double "w" as a "w" and not the Germanic "v." Go ahead, try it, no one's listening. Weird, eh? For that matter, a "wine welt" sounds like a uniquely Sonoman affliction, like something you'd discover after a night of imbibing but below the belt. You'll wish you used a "screw cap."

Though I'm grateful for Google's help with translation, I resent its facility for revealing the truth. No longer can

I explain to unassuming journalists that M.G. Vallejo founded Sonoma and then went on to form the British sports car company that happens to bear his initials. Nor can I tell them that the Historic Sonoma Plaza was once a cemetery and that City Hall was built from the gravestones. Yep, a quick online search reveals there were never bodies in the Plaza (they're in the vineyards).

"But," you say, "Daedalus, you're Sonoma's 'lifestyle ambassador,' how could you lie like a Napa wein-hure?" (Mispronounce it out loud, it's awesome.) Here's my answer: There's a dearth of "sellable" stories about Sonoma Valley. Sure, we've got the Bear Flag Revolt and were seminal in the advent of this "California" thing but to quote my editor, "What have you done for me lately?" This is what I suggest:

Push the alien agenda by claiming to have crop-circles in our vineyards. The Area 51 crowd will flock to wine country in search of intelligent life and lest we sorely disappoint them, we shall use pithy and pro-boozer slogans like "You can't spell 'saucer' without 'sauce'" or "How much wine fits in a Space Case?"

Consider the "DYI DUI." The crafting and do-it-yourself movements are growing exponentially; so will their wine tabs if we permit drunk-driving on the Plaza at least one day a year but only for those who make their own cars – out of corks. It's a virtuous circle: To build their cars they have to drink wine to get the corks to build the cars. Brilliant.

Declare war on Petaluma. Since Napa's vino-industrial complex would waste us in, like, five minutes, we have to pick on a rival we're sure to beat – find me a Petaluma winery and I'll show you envy in a bottle. Petaluma's collective ego is as weak as its one-time claim to fame as "Egg Basket of the World." Losers. "Butter and Egg Day

Parade?" How about "Cholesterol on a Float?" Simply put, Petaluma is trying to kill you with heart disease, which red wine is scientifically proven to combat. We've got that in Sonoma and plenty of it. What do you have Petaluma, a free ride to a coronary? Thanks, but I'll take a cab. Get it?

For my next trick, ladies and gewürztraminer, I'm producing a video entitled "Sonoma Valley Secrets," which sounds more like a tell-all about local bed-hopping than a travelogue. That said, I seek your input – otherwise, I'll just make some crap up.

Artisanal is the New Xtreme!

I've long thought that the term "artisan" and its shifty cousin "artisanal" should be thrown up against the hard wall of semantics and brought in on jargon charges. It's most often used around these parts as a fifty-cent appliqué to all manner of epicurea. Take a foodstuff you love, add "artisan" to its label and $2 to its price tag. Marketing meets meshugana – make that "artisanal meshugana." Yum.

Now, a report from Napa-based business and strategy consultancy Scion Advisors declares that "Artisan is the New Quality Standard," which is sort of like calling the kettle the "new black," except this kettle is a crock and their PR firm should have known I'm the one hack in town who goes ballistic when someone tries to force feed my inbox a trend piece.

I've got no grudge with Scion Advisors – we've got some crossover in clientele and, hey, I'm a sucker for a good PowerPoint slide show crunched into a PDF, which seems to be their métier. (Like we used to say with the microscopes in biology class, "If you can get it to fit on a slide, do it," which is also why I never graduated.) To be fair, the report in question is actually entitled "Trend Watch 2011: An American Cultural Renaissance Propels New Food and Beverage Trends." It was the press release that slathered on the A-word.

Hyperbole I can handle – talk is cheap, so say it big. But for the love of God, publicists, do not tell me we're in the midst of a culinary revolution and then cite Frito-Lay's recently launched "Tostitos artisan recipes" as an example. I'm a Sonoman, even our tap water is artisanal and I can say, categorically, that anything from Frito-Lay is not. That is, unless we've expanded the word's meaning to include "partially hydrogenated oil" and "corn syrup" as part of its definition; "artful," perhaps – in the "cunning" and "sly" sense of the word (not full of "art" so much as "full of crap," literally.) But definitely not artisanal, unless you're only referring to the last four letters.

The report was penned by Scion Advisors' managing director Deborah Steinthal, who, according to the release, "came to know true artisan quality" while growing up in Belgium. Apparently, she also grew accustomed to the delivery of Stella Artois with the daily dairy, which is exceptionally cool and likely why she suffered "culture shock" when she moved to the states in the 1970s. I was born here in the 70s and I too remember a pervasive sense of culture shock. The decade was a mess, particularly for food, some of which became inextricably linked to death: Kool-Aid at Jonestown and Dan White's frickin' Twinkie Defense. Of course, those of more artisanal palates might ask if a powdered drink mix and a cream-filled tube with a 20-year shelf-life qualifies as food at all. Permit me to reply by offering a Tostito.

"She was unable to stomach this new cuisine, to say the least," the release further explains. So, did she starve to death? Was she suffering from some sort of xenophobic anorexia, or, would that be "Xenorexia?" (Sounds like an evil planet, or a nightclub – let's go.) She lived. And is pleased as punch (not Kool-Aid), given the "great shifts in American values, culture and eating habits, it's a flashback to my childhood in Europe." The release also acknowledges "$6 cupcakes" as a sign of America's deepened commitment to artisanal notions, though I think it's more of a commitment to capitalism. And when did the "$6 cupcake" sneak into the pastry case? Is it a new form of cupcake next to red velvet and lemon-berry? And how does a $6 cupcake taste? Artisanally, naturally.

Real Sonoman Test

The term "real" is thrown around willy-nilly as pertains to notions of authenticity in Sonoma. "Real Sonoma," "Real Wine Country," or even, "Will the real M.G. Vallejo please stand up?" The point is, the word has become virtually meaningless – I mean, as recently as the first of this month Pepperidge Farms, Inc., was issued a "notice of allowance" by the trademark office for the term "Sonoma" – is that "Real Sonoma?" The goldfish cracker people? Really? (And who's minding our intellectual property rights down at City Hall? This is for real.)

To combat incessant poaching of our name and likeness, our "realness" if you will, I propose a simple questionnaire devised to determine those who may call themselves or their product Sonoman versus the insidious bastards who claim provenance by proxy because they passed through on their way to hell.

Admittedly, the questions below are difficult – it took me several tries to answer them correctly myself and I wrote them. As with any test, preparation is key. Ditto sobriety (but not as much as you might need for, say, a driver's exam.) To put yourself in the frame of mind best suited for passing this quiz, repeat the following mantra: "I am a Sonoman but it's not my fault." And, yes, you will be graded.

What lies beyond the easternmost border of the City of Sonoma? A) "The Old Country." B) "New York." C.) "Napa, but you didn't hear it from me."

What is an "Alcade" or 'Alcadessa?" A) A party for a 15 year-old girl. B) An honorary title bestowed by the City. C) "I have no frickin' idea and who cares but the person they give the shiny stick to?"

Why do we have two sets of streets with the same numbers for names? A) We don't, there's just a huge mirror in the middle of the Plaza. B) So the West side can pretend to be equal to the East side. C) The original plan to have concentric "circle streets" was scrapped midway when the Plaza turned out square.

The official name of the Historic Sonoma Plaza is A) The Historic Sonoma Plaza. B) The Square. C) "I swear I parked my car here – I just can't remember which side, officer."

The Sonoma Valley anthem is A) "Wine, Wine, Wine" by the Bobby Fuller Four. B) Anything played by the Whiskey Thieves at last call. C) Doing the alphabet backwards.

The stretch of Highway 12 that passes through Boyes Hot Springs is also known as A) "Blood Alley," B) "Where the Sidewalk Ends" or C) "Sonoma Highway," a "feel good" name created for tourists who otherwise wouldn't stop until Santa Rosa.

You are part of Sonoma's gentry if A) Your name is on a winery. B) Your name is on a street sign. C) Your name is on a "summons to appear."

Extra credit: What percentage of "family-owned" wineries are actually owned by large corporations? A) More than we know. B) All of them. C) Trick question – families are corporations, duh.

Okay, class – put down your pencils. If you fail, zip up your fanny pack and get back on the tour bus. If you pass, congrats, you're one of 41,300 people in the Valley who only have to look in the mirror to see the real Sonoma.

Tasting Rooms vs. Taverns, A Primer

"Wine bars" are the hallowed grounds upon which many of Sonoma's intoxication rituals occur, so it is with great reverence that we must elucidate the difference between them and the run-of-the-mill watering hole.

First off, wine people have all but outlawed the use of the word "hole" in relation to their beloved beverage since the term "bunghole" was appropriated by cartoon potty-mouths Beavis and Butt-Head in the mid-90s. The situation had near-devastating consequences for the cooperages that produce wine barrels into which bungs, or plugs, are inserted into what are now referred to as bung-orifices (which is slightly worse in my opinion.)

To most people, the notion of a "wine barfly" is patently absurd. Those people apparently have yet to visit Sonoma, where most of our citizens would handily qualify – with pride. A wine barfly doesn't merely linger around tasting rooms staining their teeth and chatting up tourists – they often know the winemakers, can discuss ad nauseum the provenance of the wine and rightly believe they're supporting the local economy. All true. And they crawl home every night with the satisfaction that the ritual sacrifice of their livers, brain cells, and bank accounts have more direct benefit to our community than any local social program upon which they will eventually become dependent. Vicious circle or virtuous cycle? I'm happy to contribute to the people of Sonoma any way I can and being a wine barfly best suits my schedule (I mean, no one really gets anything done after 2 p.m. anyway.) So, set them up, Joe, I've got a story to tell...

Many tasting rooms on the Historic Sonoma Plaza offer the enological equivalent to armchair travel. Don't have time to tour every nook and cranny of Sonoma's bustling wine country? Pull up a stool and take a tour of the tasting menu – it's the same juice with none of the trouble of trying to park your car between those damn white lines.

In fact, some wineries have a smattering of tasting rooms strategically located throughout the valley so as to catch visitors at every level of intoxication. In my experience, it's best to work one's way into the valley toward the Plaza where a park bench awaits with your name on it. My name, for example, is literally carved into the bench – I believe I gnawed it into the wood with my teeth in case I died in the night and needed to be identified. Where was my wallet, you ask? Once those things are empty they're worthless, so I tossed it in a tasting room spit bucket, if memory serves.

If you're a few too far along and aren't sure whether you're in a wine bar or have lowered the bar, so to speak and have found yourself in a bar-bar (sounds like Babar the Elephant's Bostonian sister,) there are a few clues that can orient you. Check and see if there's a bouncer. Most Sonoma joints have someone working the door – if that person offers you a bit of bread to dip in a little paper cup of olive oil, you're in a wine bar (or a roughneck dive in Napa.) If the person at the door throws you into traffic should you ask "Where's the olive oil, man?" you're at a real bar. If you're so drunk you're drinking little cups of olive oil, you're at my house and we've grabbed the wrong bottle – again.

Tasting Room Etiquette

I have had the pleasure of visiting hundreds of tasting rooms and have mastered the etiquette such that the managers themselves will often escort me to the door after a hearty afternoon of throwing back tastes. Yes, I am a professional.

The tasting room protocols we use today hearken back to the first tasting room, the Forum Vinarium of ancient Rome, located next door to the Forum Vomitorium. Yet, the same dilemmas persist, such as the ubiquitous "Spit or swallow?" This question has plagued many wine enthusiasts since their first communion. A good rule of thumb is to do what you do in the privacy of your own home. If you swallow at home, swallow in the tasting room. If you choose to spit, there is always the spit-bucket, or as we call it in Spain, the "sangria."

Complimentary tastings or "comps," from a Latin term meaning "to beg in reverse," are a frequent fringe benefit for those of us in the wine trade. If you're not in the grape game you can easily appear to be by introducing yourself as a member of one of a number of noted wine dynasties. Names like Mondavi, Ernest or Julio, and Welch's are some of the many associated with grapes. If it's true that we all share a common ancestor (the so-called "Grandpa Darwin Theory,") then it's likely that you were related to someone at some time who was in wine – you might even be an heir. I, for example, have long held the assumption that the

Howell Mountain appellation in Napa is named for some forgotten ancestor of mine. And someday, I'm going to get it back.

If, however, you're not a member of the family of Man but still feel worthy of a comp, simply say you're a member of the media (this works for me every time.) At this point in my storied career, of course, simply saying "Daedalus Howell" is now enough to garner free vino (or frino, as we say,) seeing as my name has come to be synonymous with journalistic integrity and cultural refinement. Theoretically, saying that you're "Daedalus Howell" could work for you, too (to apply for an official Daedalus Howell Franchise Kit, email my publisher.) I find opening with a pithy line usually breaks the ice. A rhetorical question such as "Do you know who I am?" works well, since it segues nicely into saying my name.

Now that you're a wine writer, it's important to keep the wine flowing for the sake of your research. Remember, the past participle of "drink" is "drunk" and writers are known for their grammar. To keep it flowing, be sure to refer to the tasting room attendant with respect – terms like "bartender" and "boy" are effective, as is the traditional "wine wench" if your attendant is a woman. If you call a female attendant "wench" and she splashes wine in your face – congratulations! You've just been initiated into the inner circle of wine connoisseurs. I can still taste the briney blend of joyful tears and a piquant gamay noir from my own initiation.

Sonoma Media Echo Chamber

I'm not too proud to admit it took me 15 minutes to realize that "#SOTU" was the Twitter hash-tag for Tuesday's "State of the Union." I was too busy trying to decipher J.M. Berry's tweets to follow the President's speech through the proxy of 140 characters. Of course, Berry's own commentary reads like a typography salad that requires a few cranks of the Enigma machine to decrypt. Defeated, I went back to "#SOTU," which I figured was some hip Japanese noodle craze I'd missed since I never eat anything I find on the Internet. It is, after all, a "cesspool" according to some pundits.

Sonoma must have its hip waders on, for cesspool or not, Sonoma is deep in the digital mire as one of the most well represented communities on the Internet. There are a dozen or so websites that now complement its media ecosystem, proffering information from hard news to tips on what wine to bring to a fistfight.

Among the NKOTB (yes, I just used an 80s boy-band acronym) is Sonoma.Patch.com, the local iteration of the AOL-backed community news site that recently made its local bow. Ditto the *New York Times*-driven "YouTown" initiative, which also boasts a Sonoma edition. This, of course, is in addition to the sites of our local newspapers and a smattering of other homegrown initiatives telling Sonoma's stories via pixel like so many bubbles in a glass of Gloria. Why the sudden flurry of interest in Sonoma by media companies great and small? Well, in the case of the venerable 135-year-old *Index-Tribune*, "sudden" might not be the most accurate notion but there has certainly been an up-tick in local online coverage the past five years. The reasons are myriad – the barrier to entry is nil, everyone's an "expert" and Sonoma is intrinsically interesting not least because we're all here (well, I'm in hiding, but that's beside the point.)

Likewise, there's a misapprehension among a certain sort of media huckster that we're early adopters. We're not. We'd still be pulling corks out with our teeth had some tourist not left a winged corkscrew on a Plaza picnic table back in the 70s. Even then, everyone first thought it was a lewd jumping-jack toy. Perhaps we're serving as some sort of test market – media guinea pigs let loose upon an ever-expanding proving grounds. This is about as palatable to some locals as the Tuskegee syphilis experiments of the 30s, wherein citizens were injected with the disease under some diabolic pretense for the sake of science.

For the record, Sonomans are perfectly capable of getting syphilis on their own, let alone local news, which, given the size of this town, they're apt to have made themselves. I mean, how many times have you thumbed through the latest edition after a wild weekend to see if you made it into the police blotter? It's damn near a rite of passage here.

This hyper-local coverage trend can lead to a kind of homespun myopia. Here we have the greatest communications tool ever invented in the history of humankind, one that can connect us to the world at large and most everybody in it and yet we're more interested in our backyard. Surely, this is why I mistook the State of the Union for a noodle. I'll look for future Sonoma news on Twitter with the hash-tag #sonomamediaechochamber.

Flu

Beware, Sonoma, a nasty flu is loose in our fair burg and it's got your name on it. No, it's not the so-called "Sonoma Flu," which conveniently afflicts people after wine-soaked weekends and necessitates sheepish calls to the office. This one is the real deal – a bilious offense upon one's intestines that, as Eric Idle quipped whilst reviewing Australian table wine, "Really opens up the sluices on both ends."

Having experienced this horrific virus myself this week, I can only assume that it was borne of A) science fiction; B) Al qaeda; or C) Some kind of disturbed-tomb-related curse. Whatever its origin, this gastro-intestinal Armageddon is as disgusting as it is violent and may require one to build a Roman-themed addition to one's home – the vomitorium (hey, it's no weirder than your "man cave" or as they called it in ancient Rome, the "masturbatorium.")

When I was a boy, being sick meant staying home from school, watching *Leave it to Beaver* reruns, and grubbing on Campbell's chicken noodle soup and saltine crackers. For an eight-year-old in the 80s, cuddled up, clutching a Darth Vader action figure in one hand and sniffing a cherry-scented felt tip marker with the other, this was essentially heaven. It's no wonder I thought the Beav' was the bomb – I was getting high with the dark side. But I was also getting well soon. As an adult, being sick means lost productivity (so long, wages, paid time off, client confidence) and nagging reminders of one's own mortality in a chaotic and uncaring universe.

The only upside of this super-flu, if one can perceive such a silver lining amongst the vapors, is the dropping of a pant size or two, since one's intake-to-output ratio dramatically skews toward the latter. However, I would no sooner recommend this flu for weight-loss than I would chewing the muzzle of a shotgun for dental hygiene. It's a killer and to be avoided at all costs – here's two ways to do so:

Avoid tourists. Who knows where they've come from and what they've got? Think about it – there's a reason no one wants them at home. It's the dead of winter, they're not on vacation, they've been quarantined. You think they came to Sonoma to see our vineyards? The vineyards just look like rows of sticks right now and you can see rows of sticks anywhere. These people are diseased exiles who spent six hours breathing infected, recycled air on a crammed jetliner and are now taking advantage of our hospitality and repaying us with the space-flu. Sure, they're good for our local economy but so is having a workforce that's not transfusing Pepto-Bismol.

No spitting. Seriously, there's nothing more vile and irresponsible than spitting in public. If you must spit, wear a bag on your head and keep your single-serve germ-warfare to yourself. For those into gross-out scenes, spend half an hour people-watching on the Historic Sonoma Plaza. You will witness that the square is really a huge Petri dish of human expectorate. Nearly one out of five dudes (and yes, it's all dudes) find it perfectly sensible to leave little toxic puddles of their own effluence all over the place. There should be a law against this and if there is a law, it should be better enforced. If one of these Sonomanids spit on a tourist (or worse, if a tourist spit on them,) downtown would suddenly look like the police department parking lot. It's only a matter of time, so let's do some preventative policing. The Centers for Disease Control and Prevention will thank you. Of course, we could just let the Plaza fester and instead all enjoy the space-flu together. Then tourists will flock to Sonoma to visit the only vomitorium on the National Registry of Historic Sites.

The Isle of Sonoma

No man is an island. However, if he lives in Sonoma, he may well be on one – or at least isolated on an inland isle with his fellow Sonomans, or, if you're feeling fancy, marooned on an existential archipelago with fellow philosophers and philistines, just west of Napa.

Yes, I know that both geographically and geologically speaking Sonoma technically isn't an island, but the Petaluma River isn't technically a river either and no one seems to have noticed (It's a tidal estuary, which we natives pronounce "slough.") Sonoma, as we know, can be an island of the mind, ringed by a moat of merlot that's content to continue on its own merry way until the cows come Rhône.

Ask yourself the following questions:

When is the last time you visited a major metropolitan city (and, no, Santa Rosa doesn't count)? Besides our local media, how often do you consume media from international sources (our local Spanish language broadcasts don't cut it?)

And if a Sonoman actually escapes the city limits and finds themselves fine dining on a business trip or on vacation, they will peruse the wine list for Sonoma wines and either disparage the restaurant for not carrying them or ruefully order one and lament the inevitable markup.

You can see where this is going and I can be snarky about it because I've been there. Or, to be more precise, I've been here, for "there" is such an abstract concept I can barely conceive of it in a single thought. This is because my prefrontal cortex is a withered nub of formerly grey matter that's now a garnet blotch thanks to our homegrown vino. This is for the better, as it keeps my editors employed correcting my frequent mispellings.

Why is it so many Sonomans find it so easy to become citywide shut-ins? Sure, it's Shangri-La and all that crap but it can also be like an episode of "The Prisoner" inter-cut with "Groundhog Day" and a self-hypnosis tape-loop of "Agoraphobia for Dummies."

Give us a few thousand years and we'll begin to speciate from the rest our kin like blue-footed boobies in the Galapagos. If we started crushing grapes with our feet again, we'd already be there. Or perhaps we're in the midst of devolution back to simpler minds? We'll be too dumb to know, though the Sonoma jokes I've heard around the water-cooler are at least worth a self-deprecating chuckle.

How many Sonomans does it take to screw in a light bulb? *One, but only after you explain it turns the same way as a corkscrew.*

How many Sonomans does it take to pick a grape? *None, until someone calls Immigration.*

What's the difference between Sonoma County and Sonoma Valley? *Sonoma County thinks it's Sonoma Valley and Sonoma Valley thinks it's Napa.*

What does S'noma stand for? *Speak Not Of My Alcoholism.*

A Napan, a Marinite, and a Sonoman walk into a bar. The Napan orders a magnum of an expensive cult cabernet and glasses for everyone in the joint. The Marinite does the same and also throws a kilo of cocaine on the bar and announces "Free for one and all!" The Sonoman drinks all the wine, snorts the entire kilo and then bums a cigarette off a passing teenager. When the Napan and Marinite suggest it's time to go, the Sonoman sighs and says, "Well, that was a fast lunch hour."

For fear that the adage "every joke has a grain of truth" is not a joke and true – at least at a granular level – let's keep this one amongst us Sonomans. Some things that are better kept in town – you know, like a quarantine. The question is, does our little island colony keep the world safe from us – or does it keep us safe from the world?

This is the type of Sonoman that I never thought I'd become. The one that brags to visiting friends, "…Another thing that's so bloody great about Sonoma is how close we are to the City. Heck, we can go anytime we want!" But we don't.

The city in this scenario, of course, is San Francisco – that gleaming seven-by-seven mile metropolis, which from Sonoma Plaza to toll plaza is but a scant 39.6 miles south. So near is the City by the Bay, that some lucky Sonomans can actually see it from their hillside homes, weather permitting. And, somehow, they don't go there either.

Clearly, I'm not speaking of Sonoma's few brave commuters who make the daily drive by car, carpool, or daisy-chain of public transit, to toil toward a tax bracket that makes it all worthwhile. I'm referring to the islanders, those of us for whom traveling south of Schellville is a pilgrimage on par with a trip to Hell.

But why? We are not provincial people. We're not a bunch o' grape-stompin' hillbillies, for the most part. Are we bridge averse? Wary of earthquakes? Or did we just forget how to get there? I know I nearly did during a trip I forced myself to take this week. To spare my fellow Sonomans the embarrassment of also having to ask the kid at the coffee cart how to get out of town, below are instructions made specifically for Sonomans that you may clip, tweet, or tattoo backward on your forehead so you can read them in the rearview mirror.

A) Starting from the Historic Sonoma Plaza, do not pass "Go," do not "Collect $200," just head south down Broadway.

B) Turn right at Hwy 121. Ignore the voice in your head doing the sci-fi TV show monologue: "You are about to participate in a great adventure. You are about to experience the awe and mystery which reaches from the inner mind to the outer limits." If it's not the *Twilight Zone*, you're fine.

C) Turn left at Arnold and proceed toward Infineon Raceway, which, despite oodles of time and money spent on branding, Sonomans still call Sears Point.

D) Turn right at Sears Point onto Hwy 37.

E) Exit onto Hwy 101, otherwise known on this stretch as "Redwood Highway," you know, because of the redwood trees that (used to) line it. Interestingly, the highway has six additional official names, including "Hollywood Highway," where it fittingly reaches its terminus in a flotilla of smog. Be sure to keep left at the fork, by the way, or you'll end up in the Novato Narrows or, worse, Petaluma.

F) Cross the Golden Gate Bridge. You'd be amazed at how many Sonomans scurry off to Sausalito at the last exit before the bridge or get themselves hung up at Vista

Point and lament how they've never been to Alcatraz. Get on the bridge. Stay on the bridge. Look to your right and wave to Japan. Look to your left and wave to the opposing traffic – they love it.

G) Pay the toll. It's $6. Do not act shocked or surprised otherwise everyone will know how infrequently you make it to the City. Do not attempt to tip or otherwise patronize the tollbooth personnel. They are officially known as "bridge officers" for a reason.

H) Turn around immediately and return to Sonoma. Seriously, I mean, come on, San Francisco? Been there, done that, right? Besides, you can go anytime.

So-no-man is an island.

Don't Drive into an 'Auld Lang Syne' Post

New Year's Eve annually conspires to reduce many Sonomans into blithering, alcohol-infused morons. Worried you've gone over the edge? Of course you are. Fret no more – use this very column to accurately test your level of sobriety. Instructions: A) Clip the column (or if reading online, print, then clip); B) Roll the column into a tube about the width of a cigarette; C) Blow into the tube; D) Repeat five times. Now, if you followed any of the preceding instructions, you are intoxicated. If you got as far as D and found yourself actually blowing into a rolled-up newspaper column, you are definitely well over the line, especially if you repeated the exercise all five times. This is an indication that you should head to bed immediately and await your first hangover of 2011. You've earned it.

Now, if you awake in Sonoma and are not in a coma or dead but are generally dissatisfied with how you feel due to over-consumption, here's a fix – resume drinking until you are in a coma or dead. Though this will end your hangover, it is not generally recommended, as it will also take much of the joy out of the New Year for you, those who care about you, and the publishers of this column who have come to depend on your readership.

There are, however, several ways to avoid death this New Year's – paramount among them is to never, ever, under any circumstances, get behind the wheel of a car while intoxicated. Getting under the wheel of a car while intoxicated is another matter entirely, which will be addressed in a subsequent column.

Among the surefire ways not to find oneself driving drunk is to NOT DRINK as well as NOT DRIVE; though it's been scientifically proven that invoking either of these acts of civic responsibility will suffice. "Driving while intoxicated" or as we say in California with echoes of Cassavetes, "driving under the influence," is not only preventable, it's the law in both the legal and cosmic sense.

Admittedly, simply chiding Sonoma on the evils of drunk driving would be hypocritical of me. Though I've never received a DUI, there have certainly been times that one would have been warranted, which I'm neither proud to share nor believe is conduct befitting someone who enjoys the privilege of bending the public ear. So, I've modified my behavior. Yes, it was that easy. Moreover, I know I'm not alone in this admission – it's something many Sonomans have done and have witnessed others do with half-hearted queries of "Are you sure you're alright?" and a kiss goodnight.

In Sonoma, it's been my observation that it's not a question of "if" but "when" one will get a DUI . This is not a rite of passage I care to take and I heartily recommend the same to you dear reader(s). Statistically speaking, one of you will likely get picked up this weekend, either on the side of the road, or off the road with a shovel, thanks to a blood-alcohol level for which you alone are responsible.

I have no idea who you are but let's pretend this piece is a time machine. Let's say that you've decided to drink and drive (and, mind you, it IS a decision) and the predictable legal, financial, and medical fallout has occurred. In those seconds after your life has been irreparably altered, likely affecting others in ways too unbearable to consider, you un-roll this column (presuming you still have hands) and flash back to this moment, here and now, in which you are reading these very words – when there's still time to change the course of events that led to your DUI and the tragedy that surrounds it. Well, kiddo, this is that moment. Let's make some arrangements, plan a rideshare, designate a driver, jot down some cabbie numbers… Yes, it's that easy. Your future self thanks you for a much happier New Year.

Vern's Taxi (707) 938-8885
Bear Flag Taxi (707) 938-1516
Sonoma County Coroner's Office (707) 565-5070

Sonoma Holiday Tips

Every winter, a certain cadre of my brilliant readers clamor for advice on how to navigate the holiday season without getting fat or going broke. They remember arriving in Sonoma both thin and rich and now desire a Christmas just like the ones they used to know. Ha-ha-ha. I mean, Ho-ho-ho.

Here's how to avoid holiday weight gain – forgo food entirely and subsist entirely on wine. The average human can survive 28 days without food, whereas the average Sonoman will last only a weekend without wine. Ergo, I suggest that Sonomans drink only wine for the next 28 days. This will keep you lean and mean (and drunk) through the New Year. Yes, this might lead to liver failure but chances are your liver is already failing, so buck up and uncork a slimmer you.

Also, you might consider that the Sonoma Diet franchise proffers its own wine brand, "The Sonoma Diet Wine Collection" produced by Windsor Vineyards, which, in my opinion, is both an offense to dieting and wine. I'd rather eat a cork, at least it would have some fiber. But a wine with the word "Diet" on the label? Look what's being done in our name. If I wanted a "lite" wine, I'd pour myself a glass of water and wait for Jesus to show up and fix it.

Whenever a denizen of wine country is invited to a

holiday party outside our borders, this is a subtle social cue to bring wine. Yes, everyone expects it and yes they have the errant notion that it's somehow free for us as if we bottle it at the banks of the ever-flowing River O'Wine that winds through our backyards. Though this is true and we mustn't ever let our secret be known, things get awkward unless we oblige. Friends have a nasty habit of reminding us that they paid for all the illicit substances one ingested back in the 80s so it's only fitting we now pay for the wine. Hmm. Fortunately, Sonoma wine is becoming so ubiquitous, you can pop by your friend's or relative's local bottle shop minutes before arriving. When they ask how you managed to keep the sauvignon blanc chilled during your four-hour drive over the hills and through the woods, tell them Jack Frost kept it on his lap.

Anyone who has ever presented a bottle of wine as a gift knows it's impossible to wrap. Several innovations in years past, from slender totes to boxes festooned with bows, have attempted to address the issue with limited success. The wine gift merely looks like a gussied up after-thought, which, let's face it, it is. When you learned that so-and-so was going to be wherever it is you're going, you ran to the wine fridge and plucked a bottle that was almost as good as the one that first came to mind. You've most assuredly both given and received such bottles, which invariably come with the proviso "Let this one lay down for a while, open it in a year or two and it will be excellent." This is code for "Don't bother drinking this plonk – re-gift at your earliest convenience – like I did."

For those near and dear to me, a brown bag usually suffices since they generally want to twist off the cap and get down to the Plaza before the spirit of Christmas passes (leaving a headache and regret in its wake.) By far the most awesome wrapping for a wine gift is to acquire a three-mast ship and place the bottle in the hull – a grand gesture that reverses the "ship in a bottle" gag to the nth degree. Of course, the recipient will just tear the ship apart to get to the present, paying no heed to the wrapping.

But then, what counts is on the inside, right? No matter how fat and broke you are.

Sonoma's Secret Societies

I received an email from the Sonoma Valley Vintners and Growers Alliance today and happily clicked through because I like my spam paired with wine and (full disclosure) the organization is a client of mine. In it was an invitation to join the Sonoma Valley Grapes and Wine Society, which affords one all sorts of amenities and exclusive arrangements devised to complement one's wine country lifestyle. Seeing as my schedule leaves more style than an actual life at present, my societal needs are a mite bit more circumspect. I'm more inclined to join a "secret society," one where no one knows anyone, never shows up anyway and pays dues directly to me. You can join but you must first file an application fee. How much? It's a secret. Pick a number and I'll tell you if it needs to be higher. And trust me, it needs to be higher.

Sonoma is chockablock with secret societies. Pick any proclivity, profession, or passion and there are likely a few souls huddled around a candle, going through the motions of some ritual baloney in a wine cave near you. Weird? Sure. But effective – secret societies have long been a means to get business done, particularly when it comes to creating puppet governments or re-jiggering the banking system. They're also good for getting one drunk.

"Press Club" was my gang's ill-fated attempt at a secret

society, which failed miserably because, A) journalists can't keep a secret and B) we were overly social and well-lubricated in so doing. Turns out, drinking and writing only go well together in the movies, and our society began to fray faster than you could order a "dyslexia and soda." Also, our password was "swordfish," which accounted for the Marxists who frequently overran us (ever try to clean a greasepaint mustache off a pint glass?).

Among Sonoma's other secret societies is my fan club. I bet. I mean, I know they're out there yet no one publicly claims membership – the better to protect the shrine to me, I suppose. In fact, I communicate to them through this column – take the first letter of every sentence and decipher the anagram. I don't mind revealing how to do this, for only true secret society fan club members would bother to take the time. But you non-secret-society-fan-club members are thinking about it now, aren't you? That's the first step in the initiation process, which is followed by the "passing of the cash," an ancient ritual that involves large bills, a paper bag, and a secret drop location.

Of course, the best secret societies are those that come with a decoder ring and a membership badge. I'm personally a fan of any group whose sacred accoutrements can be found in a box of Cracker-Jacks. The ones that require blood oaths, pledges to supernatural characters, or the occasional assassination, not so much. Do such shadowy and clandestine groups rule Sonoma? Meh. Would it be cool if they did? Yes, but only in the motion picture version. It would be "The Da Vinci Code" meets "Sideways" with a little "Eyes Wide Shut" and "Dead Poets Society." It would consist of a single scene of Sonomans reading cryptograms aloud, in a wine cave, naked, while emphatically not drinking merlot. Typical weekend, really.

If your secret society wants to bankroll this film do not bother the Sonoma Film Society – bother the Secret Sonoma Film Society, a shadow operation that hosts the Secret Sonoma Film Festival. The group is so secretive it's said even the credits are expunged from the films they screen. No one knows who the members are, not even the members. Sometimes, members don't even know they are members. I know I don't and if I did, I couldn't tell you.

Wherefore Fall?

For chaps like me, those who put the twee in tweed and refer to themselves as chaps whilst writing pithily for a 130-year-old institution, Fall is the saison d'etre. Throw in some elbow patches and a pipe stuffed with black cavendish as rain lightly drums the window and you get the picture.

Apparently, the Weather disagrees. Clearly, it didn't get the memo about the Autumnal Equinox last week – a typical bureaucratic snafu and one that has resulted in triple digit temperatures at the tail-end of September. It's Fall, damn it – where's the must of antiquarian books, itchy wool scarves, and warm apple cider? Incinerated by the heat, I assume.

Even autumnal sounds, like the crunch of leaves beneath muddy boots, have been replaced by, say, the sound of an egg sizzling on the sidewalk. How is it one can fry an egg on the sidewalk in Fall? I've no idea but I know an ex-veep with PowerPoint who can explain it.

Why would anyone in Sonoma want to fry an egg in on the sidewalk anyway? Oh, that's right, because they can. In the Springs, Sonoma's bastard half-sister where sidewalks are few and far between (like, between a highway and a hard place) you can only fry an egg on the side of the road. The result is less egg and more bottle cap and cigarette butt omelet. But the fact remains, you could do it if you desired. The Weather, however, still scorches every grape on the vine.

A colleague of ours reportedly placed a sheet of unbaked cookies in the rear window of her car and giddily returned to find the dough baked and cookies warm to the touch. As charming and inventive as I find the way she embraced the heat-wave with open oven mitts, I cannot help but think she is somehow baiting the Weather gods do something truly heinous. Like turn our town into a smoking pile of ash. Something tells me this woman would bring marshmallows to the inferno, however. And a very, very long stick.

Though we are frequently chided by public service announcements to not cook our canines and kids in parked cars, people still do. Please don't. Without the A/C cranked, our cars are ovens in the waiting. Just because your SUV looks like a Viking range on wheels doesn't mean you are permitted to cook in it. We have taco trucks for that. Besides, it's bad for the upholstery. You ever try to get Baked Alaskan off leather interior? I have and it ain't pretty. The meringue bonds with the seats on a molecular level only to randomly remove itself whenever your spouse happens to sit there, which leads to the inevitable reprise of "What the hell were you doing with a Baked Alaskan in your car anyway?" Like climate change – it's complicated.

To simulate what Autumn once was for my one-year-old son, The Cannoli, I bundle him up in corduroy, put him in his car seat, crank the air-conditioning and spray water on the windows while rustling a box of potpourri, which is my "crunch of leaves beneath muddy boots" sound effect. He isn't impressed. Touring him through the automatic carwash – my upcoming winter simulation – however, should be a hit. After the "storm," we'll don shorts and tank tops and go fry an egg on the East side. And next Summer, when he's two, we'll celebrate his birthday in the Plaza in shiny new fire-retardant suits while waiting for his birthday cake to finish baking in the car.

Staycation Wonderland

It's been observed that our tourists seem to enjoy themselves in our town more than we Sonomans. This perception could be the result of many factors, not least of which being that tourists can afford to enjoy themselves in Sonoma's wine country, whereas we Sonomans spend all of our money merely trying to live here.

I suppose one could say that, as residents, we're on some kind of "permanent vacation" in our "destination location" but unless you're in a Jim Jarmusch film, an Aerosmith album, or your "boyfriend's back and you're gonna get in trouble," the sentiment rings kind of hollow.

This is why the so-called "staycation" always rubs some of us like a losing lottery scratcher. Though some Sonoma wineries offer free tastings to townies, there are few other experiences that tourists and locals can both enjoy without dropping a paycheck. This is a fact of life – tourism is business, Sonoma is a tourist town, ergo Sonoma is in the business of inhaling your wallet and spitting out its empty remains like a tamale husk.

Many Sonomans are slaves to the wine country dream, which is like the American dream but served atop a bed of arugula. The iconic "white picket fence" is crushed under the weight of zinfandel vines and there's a church key beneath every "welcome" mat. Other Sonomans just woke up here one day to find a landscape that seems to have shifted beneath their very feet. Ask any local over 40 about what it was like "before" and their comments are invariably preceded by a slight shake of the head and a quiet sigh. Whatever follows is academic, they've already said volumes. Things ain't as sweet as they used to be – now they're tannic, herbaceous, and sometimes jammy.

Then there are the newbies. Some come to Sonoma to aspire, others to retire – yet another demographic comes to expire, which is admirable in its own grim way. Ironic that science (or the wine lobby) keeps finding links to imbibing and longevity. Perhaps Sonoma's expirees seek the fountain of youth in the wine that flows freely from the font of fundraisers, say, or perhaps the purple-drench is their exit made glass by glass like foundling footsteps toward their maker.

Of course, as a joke making the rounds goes, "In Sonoma you drink yourself to death, in the neighboring, comparatively low-rent Boyes Hot Springs, you drink yourself to meth." Hmm. Couldn't it have been "math?" If drinking led to better arithmetic instead of methamphetamine I would have passed algebra the first time (I passed on the meth too, by the way.) The Springs would be MIT West given all the "math." Instead of graffiti, there would be equations scrawled everywhere. Alas, the only numbers we got are the ones plummeting from the real estate appraisals.

The devastation of the home market is clearly the result of the greater economic woes affecting the nation at large rather than a mere couple of lab busts. Likewise, as any merchant might tell you, there has been a slip in what is usually a robust season for Sonoma's tourist business. Given the current fiscal climate how does one find the presence of mind to enjoy the wine country's peak season whilst the recession double-dips our collective aioli?

Slum it like a tourist. Start by strolling to any of a number of our hotel lobbies, take a seat and unfurl a newspaper (this one will do). Read absently while people-watching, until a sense of superiority begins to well in the darker recesses of your soul. When satisfied, loosely fold the paper under your arm and conspicuously adjust yourself. Meander to the Plaza, walk twenty feet, pause and look at a tree you've never noticed before. Take a deep breath. Exhale while saying "Mine."

Free Dirt

"Free dirt." That's how the sign reads on Hwy. 12. Gotta love it: Simple, direct and perhaps even effective. I wouldn't know seeing as I'm dealing with my own dirt at present, so I haven't called to ask. However, the sign is something of a roadside Zen koan.

Is it intended to read "Free dirt" in the way we think "Free beer?" or is it a plea to release dirt from the clutches of captivity? For that matter do they mean "dirt" as in soiling substance as in mud or earth, or dirt as in gossip and scandal? If the latter is the case, they may be angling to put me out of business since as me and my confederates have moved to a paid-content model. This dirt may be cheap but it ain't free (somehow "Cheap Dirt" doesn't have the same ring, though "Dirt Cheap" kind of does.)

In wine-savvy Sonoma, however, one could say the marketing genius behind the "Free Dirt" campaign is missing an opportunity. It seems that "Free Terroir" might move the merchandise a bit quicker, terroir, of course, being the special characteristics geography bestows upon the farming of grapes. In fact, a more entrepreneurial type might ascribe a value a notch or two above "free" to the pile of a 100 percent pure Sonoma Valley appellation, but then anyone rich enough to give away their dirt for free likely finds generosity its own reward.

Of course, the notion of an "Instant Vineyard Kit" has long intrigued me. Perhaps we could bag the dirt and sell handfuls of Sonoma on the open market. My fear is that Napa would dilute the biz with their own bag o' dirt scheme, which they would inevitably class up with twigs and "organic vermi-humus," otherwise known as "worm poop." Worse yet would be the French knock-off, "Sac de Terre," which just sounds inherently classier than our "Sonoma Dirt Bag."

Dirt isn't the only object one can acquire free on Sonoma's West side. There's a practice in the Springs in which I recently participated while divesting my household of some worldly possessions (I'm not going Buddhist – I don't have the stomach for it, just the belly.)

Drag any used object outside one's house, tag it "Free" and watch it disappear. It's like magic or quantum physics. It's like a wormhole opens and swallows up anything marked "free" and located within a few feet of a curb. A lounge chair, a rug and an Edward Hopper print all disappeared from my curb within minutes. The system isn't infallible, however – the lounge chair returned a day later. This, I'm assuming, was not of its own volition and I couldn't help but feel some social code had been violated. Then, just as mysteriously, the chair disappeared again.

Now, there's either a glitch with the laws of the universe or someone waffled on their interior decorating choices and someone else hasn't – or, at least, hasn't yet. I'm not convinced that the wayfaring lounge chair won't be sent on a return trip. If it does reappear, I might come to assume its handlers have misapprehended the concept of "free" as remarked upon above.

Perhaps they think they're helping the chair enjoy its newfound freedom by touring it around the Sonoma countryside. Maybe it visited the free dirt pile where together they discussed the finer points of the esprit de liberté. Or perhaps the chair and pile are plotting. I wouldn't put it past that damn chair to engage in a conspiracy to liberate its brethren of objects. Sort of gives new meaning to the phrase "the grand scheme of things" doesn't it?

Alas, getting from free dirt to pay dirt is a dirty job but someone has to do it.

Cork vs. Cap

Before we all got hip to wine country, life's choices were relatively simple – boxers or briefs, regular or decaf, Ginger or Mary Ann? In Sonoma, of course, we have "cork or cap?" as the traditional cork stopper versus the screw-cap enclosure fracas enters a new vintage.

Stirring the debate like lees is a lobbying body, which heartily advocates – as their website's name suggests – 100PercentCork.org. For non-URL-speakers that's "all cork, all the time," courtesy of the Portuguese cork industry, which supplies much of the world's wine-stoppers.

Here, I must admit that I didn't catch this lead from a wine trade magazine (I scribble for a few) or even a winemaking pal (I dribble for a few) but rather the *New York Times*, whose nose for news has been sniffing more than a few bungholes of late (anyone catch their creative geography in that recent "36 Hours in Sonoma" puff piece?)

Media and advertising columnist Stuart Elliott broke the story of the cork industry's goal to reassert itself as the stopper of choice in Tuesday's *Times* wherein he recapped efforts that include social media, a pro-cork petition, and the positioning of tree-grown corks as a "green" option. For fear of confusing the matter, the notion of "cap and trade" shall be left untapped as we explore the intersection of green themes and wine, lest we end up with an energy policy, or get drunk, or get drunk and end up with an energy policy, which is what happened during the last administration.

What's interesting to us media mavens is that flak firm Sitrick & Company and San Francisco buzz builders Citizen Group are working up the split on a $3 million budget with a cool million earmarked for advertising. That the Portuguese government and their American partners, the Sonoma County-based Cork Quality Council, managed to overlook the fine media outlets in our valley whilst making their media buys is something of a sour note. There are dozens of publications that would've happily popped a cork for a piece of that action. There are even a few that would eat a cork for a splash of cash. Or wine. One need not open the bottle to read its message: "Send money. Thanks, The Media."

The reason for the oversight could be due to Sonoma's hard-won perception as an industry town and thus not representative of the broader consumer market the cork lobby is targeting. In fact, it's openly advocating the boycott of screw-cap wines, which could be misconstrued as more anti-wine than pro-cork given our industry's recent struggles. Ultimately, it's in Sonoma's interest to sell bottles of wine, regardless of how they're plugged. We should just be grateful our wine is in bottles rather than boxes. Who wants to discuss the relative merits of a plastic spigot?

Here are some points to consider in the "Cork v. Cap" debate:

A) Yea, corks! There are few sounds more pleasing than their pop when plucked from the bottle. However, if you've never witnessed sommelier Christopher Sawyer open a screw cap by running the bottle's neck down his sleeve, spinning the cap into the air and catching it with the flick of the wrist – you haven't truly lived in Sonoma. (The trick: discretely crack the cap's seal with a good twist so that it turns freely when run down your LEFT sleeve – remember, lefty-loosey – then catch it mid-air.).

B) According to the Urban Dictionary, "To pop a cap in someone's ass" is the prelude to a gunfight. Conversely, "To pop a cork in someone's ass" is a dinner party gone horribly wrong.

C) Cork: Keep in your wedding shadow-box. Screw-cap: Keep in the glove-box so the cops won't see it.

D) Cork: Pronounced backwards as "crock." Screw-cap: Unlike most things in life, it provides a sense of closure when properly screwed.

Lost Highway

Long ago, I accepted that the construction on Highway 116 might never end. Its perennial delays and eternal dust have simply become a fact of life (and occasionally death) for Sonomans. It's as if some decree from on high declared, "Ye shall not enjoy ease of passage to and from Petaluma, for Sonoma must remain an inland island, severed from the world by a moat of wine that runneth so deep as to quench the fires of Hell." Or some such nonsense.

Moreover, Highway 116 is a bit of a shape-shifter and boasts nearly as many names as Tolkien's Gandalf, who took up different handles with whomever he was consorting, be they elves or dwarves or Caltrans employees.

Coming from the Russian River, Highway 116 is known as "River Road," which, hands down, wins the prize for "total lack of creative vision in naming a highway." Through the westerly hills of Sonoma County, the highway is known variously as the Willard F. Libby Memorial Highway (for the Sebastopol native, nuclear scientist, and member of the Atomic Energy Commission, who received the 1960 Nobel Prize in Chemistry for developing carbon-dating) and Gravenstein Highway, so-named for the apple of the same name (though vineyards have supplanted much of what was once apple orchards.) There's even a stretch known among Caltrans employees as the Cotati Grade, which sounds more like slang for inferior pot than a couple miles of scenic highway.

From Petaluma, Highway 116 is essentially schizophrenic, taking on names and hairpin turns in near equal measure. Lakeville Highway, Stage Gulch Road, and Arnold Drive are all formal monikers for various parts of the 11-mile artery to Sonoma. The final leg, prior to its terminus at Highway 121, is named for erstwhile Sonoma-retiree Gen. Hap Arnold, who was likewise mixed up with atomic pursuits. The five-star general was key to getting the B-29 bomber off the ground and bore the highly classified foreknowledge that it would be eventually be used to drop the A-bomb on Japan, 65 years ago last week.

I've alternately heard our piece of the highway called the Wino Death Trap and Glutton's Run, though the body count is as often run up from the nature of the road's design itself, or apparent lack thereof, than mere DUIs gone DOA. Hence, since at least 2003, the highway has been on Caltrans' do-over docket. We're grateful, surely, but we're also nonplussed by the stymied flow of traffic into the valley, which, very often, is mandated by a middle-aged woman in a panama hat, who bears her "Slow" sign like some sort of a traffic scepter. I've come to think of her as the Crossing Guard of Karma.

Instead of merely brandishing her sign, she undulates her hands, wrists and elbows in a manner that suggests a leisurely, rolling wave – like Tai Chi by way of traffic school. The movement, however strange, is actually effective in coaxing one's foot off the pedal. I'm not sure if she's practicing roadside hypnosis or casting a spell as if she were Glinda the Good Witch on a day job. Is Caltrans dabbling in witchcraft? Who knows, but it's working. At least it works on me. Every time I cruise by, perhaps at an ill-advised speed, the woman does her traffic voodoo and suddenly my foot levitates off the accelerator and I'm suddenly quite calm.

This Shaman of the Gravel Shoulder has a way of turning MPH into TLC, which is no mean feat in this workaday world of get-up-and-go-go-go. Perhaps her ritual gestures are some kind of interpretative dance, an ancient sign language that defies translation. Or maybe it's something as obvious as "Slow down; life's not a commute; take the scenic route and take your time – we all get where we're going soon enough." Or, as translated into the language of bumperstickers: "Better to be on the road to the end than at the end of the road."

Sonoma, The Other Leading Brand

Several years ago, an article in Sonoma County's *Press Democrat* described how our county's name, Sonoma, had finally become a "brand" name associated with wine, epicurea, and good green fun. Good for us. Too bad we're not using it ourselves.

You know how if you pop a cork of bubbly in the Champagne region, of France, it's champagne? But you do the same anywhere else and it's "sparkling wine." See, that's how it starts. The French are super-vigilant about the brand identity of their most popular export. When cheaper plonk calls itself champagne, it dilutes their brand – sometimes literally.

Companies want their products to be ubiquitous, and spend millions on marketing and positioning to get there. However, at a certain level of ubiquity, your product's name can become shorthand for all products in its category (a la "champagne" – my laptop doesn't even bother auto-correcting the proper noun.) This is why Kleenex takes ads out in Writer's Digest Magazine pleading with authors to have their characters blow their noses with tissue paper when they mean tissue paper and Kleenex when they mean Kleenex.

Ditto, Xerox (see how I did that?) How many times have you Xeroxed your butt? Millions, I know. Xerox loves it when you use a Xerox machine to "Xerox" your butt, but not when you're merely photocopying your butt.

Having your brand name become a verb is only good when that verb occurs with your product. Like Googling. You can google only at Google – which is genius. No one has ever committed an act of Yahooing, which is still illegal in the South.

The article also explored why the Sonoma name has been plastered on products that have little to no relationship with county or the town of the same name. Sonoma is known for its wine – not a cigarette or a gated community in Florida – both of which use the name Sonoma. I'm from Sonoma, but I've never smoked a Sonoma while driving a Sonoma on my way to a gated community in Florida. And I'm not even going to touch "Sonoma Valley," the Crabtree & Evelyn Eau de Toilette Perfume.

The Massachusetts-based potion and lotion company offers a Sonoma-branded fragrance redolent of "flowers, woods, and ferns native to Sonoma Valley." Frankly, Sonoma smells like the Xerox machine. Their error begs for rebuttal. Perhaps we should market a perfume scented like baked beans and cod.

What's really irksome is that this company put a tiny, but telltale, trademark symbol next to "Sonoma Valley."

After some digging at the United States Patent and Trademark Office website, I ascertained that "Sonoma Valley" had been registered by Crabtree and Evelyn, Ltd. in 2002. I'm not sure how that slipped by – the guardians of Sonoma's brand equity must have been asleep at the wheels of their GMC Sonoma trucks that year.

Perhaps the idea that any of us can lay claim to the name "Sonoma" at all is absurd. Consider our predecessors, the Coast Miwok to whom Sonoma Valley was the easternmost reach of their ancestral lands – they didn't bother with malarkey like trademarks. Hey, it's not like a bunch of marauders are coming to take the village away (again), as happened in 1861 when some people filed legislative paperwork in D.C. and effectively extinguished local Indian land titles. I mean, what are trademarks but more paperwork? I mean, if you're going to deal with D.C., who wants to bother with the United States Patent and Trademark Office when Sonoma Restaurant is just a few miles away? We can trust those guys. Right?

And, yes, there is a Sonoma Restaurant in D.C. I googled it. Cresting the search result page was "Sonoma Restaurant and Wine Bar." How could this be? What order of search engine optimization wizardry had occurred? How could a restaurant in our nation's capital have anything remotely to do with Sonoma County?

I decided to call Sonoma Restaurant and Wine Bar on Pennsylvania Avenue in Washington, D.C., and demand answers. What I got, however, was an earful of on-hold music until I got Jared Rager on the line. Instead of haranguing Rager about using our county's name for his restaurant, I found myself asking for a universal discount for all Sonomans.

"I've never thought of that," Rager replied. Well, duh, no ever thinks to make a reservation for 466,741. After a bit of a chat, it seemed that Northern Californians represent a fair amount of Rager's business. Since Sonoma defines the NorCal zeitgeist, it's no wonder Rager named his joint after us. Anyway, it wasn't until I hung up on Rager that I realized how expertly I had been played. But then he's in DC. That's what they do.

That said, there are times when brand owners overreach when defending the sanctity of their brands in the market. Like the country of Portugal. Apparently, if it's not from Portugal, it's not port – it's dessert wine. At least according to the European Union. Now, port is not a region in Portugal. It's an abbreviation. The EU doesn't care, they want their member country to be happy and have made it a legal issue – if your dessert wine isn't made in the country of Portugal, it cannot bear the four-letter abbreviation of port.

Now, stateside, we have agencies that have to enforce these laws for reasons of international commerce. The

Alcohol and Tobacco Tax and Trade Bureau has to approve every label of every wine or spirit sold in our country. Consequently, local producers of port have been put in something of a situation. Some, like Peltier Station Winery in Lodi, however, have found a work-around. They simply called their winery's 2004 zinfandel dessert wine a "USB Port" and feature the iconic digital device plug design on its label.

This gimmick has landed the USB Port in magazines, blogs, and Web sites worldwide. Moreover, it's started an examination of how much dominion a region can have in terms of defending a brand identity.

Sonoma has mounted no such defense. It has essentially left the keys to the kingdom on the nightstand of the Sonoma Inn after being royally screwed by big business. And small businesses too. The Sonoma Inn is a fleabag at the corner of Bush and Van Ness in San Francisco.

One might initially assume it's a residential hotel, by which I mean a flophouse of the ilk where pensioners and burnouts share quarters with romantic visions of alcoholic writers and sadluck dames. You know, the kind of place that would boast a plaque that reads "Charles Bukowski slept here." Not to disparage the residents, or Bukowski, whom I'm sure don't need some snarky media type from a tony wine country suburb making digs at their digs. But still – did they have to use the name Sonoma?

Just so there's no confusion, when I say "Sonoma Inn," I don't mean any place of overnight accommodation in, around or even near Sonoma, such as the Sonoma Valley Inn, the Inn at Sonoma, the Sonoma Mission Inn or even the Sonoma Creek Inn. Those we can differentiate from the pretenders by virtue of the fact that they're actually in Sonoma and have never been listed, say, in the Bedbug Registry (bedbugregistry.com) where I found this post from an apparently disgruntled guest of San Francisco's Sonoma Inn:

"Yesterday, June 18, 2009, I rented a room there. One

of the residents told me they had just been inspected and were told to spray something like three times in six weeks and that they were non-compliant to that request. The bugs are alive and biting. I don't know any details other than they bite and I have raised welts on my skin that itch terribly."

And they dare put "Sonoma" in their name? Deplorable.

Of course, I had to call. On my second attempt a woman answered the phone with a wan "Hello?" I tried to confirm that I had reached the venerable Sonoma Inn and after a moment – a rather long moment – she decided that I had. I asked if she had any vacancy. After another long pause, I realized it was incumbent upon me to define "vacancy." I asked if there were "rooms available." She said no. I asked when she might have a room and she said "Maybe tomorrow." The rate? $50 plus tax.

By comparison, a real Sonoma room is anywhere between $134.99 for a king bed and complementary continental breakfast to $255 for a non-smoking room with a queen bed at the winter discount. Just for kicks, I checked Craigslist and found a "LOVELY Sonoma Studio approximately 6 blocks from Historic Sonoma Plaza" with "ample parking" and a "queen feather bed, twin bed, flat screen TV, kitchen bath with shower and tub, WI-FI" with a bonus "bottle of wine, coffee, tea and of course chocolate with your room." $160, no tax. It seems we pay a premium for bedbug abatement here in the real Sonoma.

Maybe the world is just running out of names. As a barometer, go online and note the relative dearth of wine-themed Internet domain names currently available. Entrepreneurs from hither and yon are scouring the web for names that reference vino, but don't read like supercalifragilisticexpialidocious.com (taken.)

A fellow from New Jersey is currently squatting WineChannel.com, another in Canada is awaiting the perfect moment to launch WineCzar.com.

In my observation, there is also now a scarcity of

domains with "Sonoma" embedded in them. SonomaLife. com is awaiting birth by a Santa Rosa design firm. Less sexy SonomaLifestyle.com is also incubating somewhere in cyberspace. I recently acquired SonomaWino.com in both its single and plural forms, to point to wine columns stowed on my personal site. I resorted to the wino motif after frustrating myself in a vain search for something that would portray me as a little less down-market (but, hey, honesty is the best policy, right?) I ask: Is the day far off when SonomaThis.com and SonomaThat.com collide in a web traffic jam? As of this writing those domains are available, by the way. I wager that by the time you read this that they are both gone.

I suppose we shouldn't be surprised: Sonoma has been evolving into a brand ever since entrepreneur Chuck Williams hyphened "Sonoma" to his surname and launched what would become a houseware industry giant. That was half a century ago this year and in the intervening decades the name "Sonoma" has found itself on myriad nationally marketed products and is currently fattening the bank accounts of those behind the Sonoma Diet.

Epicurean and lifestyle magazines routinely ornament their covers with Sonoma's triple vowel word-score (though it's just as often paired with our conjoined twin Napa). Some may bristle at the notion of our wine burg becoming a buzz-worthy boomtown, a town that heretofore that has largely turned its back on the world but has always kept an eye looking over its shoulder. A media colleague of mine refers to Sonoma as The Island for what she perceives to be this very mentality. Perhaps it's a bit true, but Sonoma has always been an island, one that people like to visit, tourists and corporate conquistadors alike.

Consider the Sonoma Coffee Café near the University of California, Berkeley campus. Like the students that it serves, the coffee house seems unfinished, over-eager, and misted in a verdant odor Crabtree & Evelyn might call "Aspiration." Simply put, the Sonoma Coffee Café is trying (in more ways than one) and, as happens with alarming frequency, it has appended our town's name to a premise that bears no earthly relation to Sonoma, City of.

No wonder the Sonoma Coffee Café would seem to have more than caffeine jitters when this real Sonoma County native strolled in and gently inquired about the provenance of the joint's name. After I schooled the barista as to the meaning of "provenance" (Christ, people, I got it from "Antiques Roadshow," it's not like it's French or something – or, wait…), I was discouraged to learn that she had no idea what "Sonoma" was and assumed it had something to do with coffee, "You know, like a special spoon."

A special spoon. For the past century and a half, Sonoma has honed and crafted an industry – nay, invented it! – a metaphor for artistry, maturity, and patience, for which our name should be synonymous. Wine, damn it. And this kid thinks we're a spoon. It figures – the Sonoma Coffee Café's flagship product, coffee, could be said to be the antithesis of our central metaphor seeing as coffee also comes in an instant variety.

Perhaps the mythos surrounding coffee is more attuned to the emerging culture, one that communicates in 140-character clips and darts between devices that grow more clever by the nanosecond. Indeed, after a few fits of climate change, it might behoove us to plant coffee beans in the vineyards since they will have been seared into toothpicks and raisins by then, like a third grader's depiction of a molecule. At least after that people won't look down their noses at me for drinking Sonoma's liquid bounty in the morning (if there isn't such a thing as "breakfast wine," there should be.)

It's just as well there's an ignoramus running a fake Sonoma café in the East Bay (the chain also has locations in Hauppauge, NY and Louisville, KY, though I can't speak to the respective IQs of their counter-intelligence.) Sonoma County's own namesake joints have a tendency to grow cold and bitter like an unattended cuppa. Am told the Sonoma County Coffee Company, colloquially-known as "SoCoCo" (which sounds so-so-90s I could shriek) pulled its last espresso some time ago. Heck, even the Sonoma Café and Bistro in Florida's Del Rey beach went out of business but 150 miles away in Kissimmee, FL, yet another Sonoma Coffee Café is thriving.

I did some investigating. According to some advertorial on the JavaBean Review, "A select few financially qualified individuals with business savvy and experience will enjoy the opportunity to become a Sonoma Coffee Café Area Developer and benefit through significant streams of income from multiple locations. This means higher profits for you and the profit picture in this industry is absolutely phenomenal. (Starbucks didn't open all of those stores just for fun.)"

No, they didn't. But they also didn't nick their name from a real deal community in the heart of wine country (they stole theirs from Capt. Ahab's first mate in *Moby-Dick* but you knew that).

The question looms, however – should we pool our beans and start a franchise, which could, by dint of our name, become the flagship store? The Sonoma Sonoma Coffee Café? Or are there so many redundancies in that name that we should just be happy knowing that Sonoma actually means "wine" and "community" and that the barista was probably thinking "demitasse spoon?"

Yep, sounds just like "Sonoma" and I've measured out my life in them.

Anyway, I've got a better way of re-claiming the Sonoma brand name. Like most creative types, I've got a veritable zoo of pet projects cross-breeding in the recesses of my mind. Some are born in captivity, successfully raised, and released to the wild.

Others I've had to "put down," for fear of infecting the remaining ones with their inanity. But this one is a winner. Probably.

The "Sonoma Terroir in a Baggie" notion went feral in my imagination some time back, and starved the other pet projects of my attention for a few misguided weeks. Essentially a bag of dirt, the novelty item was to be marketed as a means of owning a little bit o' Wine Country on the cheap.

For $5 you could have a Sonoma Valley appellation starter-kit for your very own micro-vineyard. Of course, I don't own any Sonoma terroir to bag. I realize I'd have a helluva time explaining myself to the business end of a vineyard manager's shotgun while shoveling a little real estate into a Ziploc. So, perhaps I'll refrain from poaching Sonoma property that isn't preceded by the word "intellectual." I mean, the difference between "brand" and "land" seems academic at this point. Both can be cultivated, both can be squatted and both are rapidly losing their meaning. They could merge and just be "bland." I mean, what's in a name? That which we call a rose by any other name would smell as sweet, be that wine or, somehow, flowers, woods and ferns.

Sonoma Wine Month

Former Governor Schwarzenegger declared September, 2009 "California Wine Month" (again). Apparently, he's never been to Sonoma where every month is "Wine Month," which is comprised of "Wine Weeks" and "Wine Days," and so on – to hours, minutes, and nanoseconds. What's the duration of a "wine nanosecond?" About the amount of time it takes to realize that declaring September "California Wine Month" is like declaring December "Reach Your Credit Limit for Jesus Month." It's going to happen no matter what stamp Sacramento puts on it.

As the Governor said in the proclamation, the fifth of its ilk in as many years, "Our wineries attract tourism and provide countless jobs for Californians" and heck, non-Californians too, but not every industry can be like our gubernatorial office, right? So, let's not acknowledge this necessary contribution, lest we arouse jealously.

As for tourism, the question always arises – is Sonoma a wine town or a tourist town? One can assume that tourists come to Sonoma for an experience other than meeting other tourists, so let's say that it's a wine town that attracts tourism. On the rare occasion that a tourist has actually arrived with the intent of hobnobbing with other tourists, we may also assume that wine will somehow be involved either as a social lubricant (read: wine allays "social anxiety disorder," so cancel that Paxil prescription and join a wine club) or as a salve for the failed tourist alone in the B&B.

"Many are also committed to serving their communities and promoting socially and environmentally responsible farming practices," said Governor of our California wineries. This is particularly true of ours in Sonoma, which have always made a positive distinction between farming and say, agribusiness. Suffice it to say, when the Monsanto Merlot and ConAgra Cabernet hit the shelves, the jig is up. Corn syrup has taken its rightful place in America's obesity epidemic, but must it sweeten our dessert wines too?

The Governor should have declared September "California 'Sonoma' Wine Month." Then perhaps we could forgive him for (choose one) A) Being governor; B) *Kindergarten Cop* C) Possibly closing down our state parks. Dude, half of downtown Sonoma IS A STATE PARK. Thanks, Arnold. Can I get you another glass of corn wine?

In the days of yore, the business lunch was an afternoon-long affair, built around a trio of martinis (not so, these days, unless you're a character on *Mad Men*, and at last glance, the width of my tie says "No"). However, in Sonoma, there is the "three bottle lunch," which is usually enjoyed by two (or less) people in the corner of a local brasserie. It's high time the Governor and I had a Sonoma style power lunch (I am, after all, Sonoma County's official lifestyle ambassador.) We'd settle into my booth at the Fig, order up a bottle of rosé (with a second bottle – another Rhone varietal, of course – at the ready.) I'd say, "Arnold, man, you're down in the polls, our kids can learn more in prison than our public schools and we're one earthquake away from being Atlantis. Let's say you do something right and turn this thing around, eh?"

"I'm listening," the Governor says as he snaps a baguette in half with his thumb and forefinger.

"You gotta change California Wine Month to Sonoma Wine Month."

"But, it's for all of Caleefornia, Daedalus," he'd reply.

"Then change the name of California to Sonoma."

The Governor smiles wryly and then rises to go to

the restroom. "I'll be back," he joshes and I pretend to laugh. Then I wait. And wait. And then the bill comes and I realize the Governor isn't coming back.

A Bottle of Buckeye

It was 70 years ago that the venerable pages of *LIFE* Magazine crowed about the "Finest Wine from American's Finest Grape District." Ohio. Albeit, it was a paid advertisement but, my, how times have changed. "America's wine grape paradise," the Lake Erie Islands, has been eclipsed by the entire state of California, let alone Sonoma's own century-and-half foray into the biz. I'm convinced that I could cultivate my own wine grape paradise in my unkempt backyard, ignore it for a season, crush the resulting fruit with my boots on and still end up with a better wine, even after I've bottled in plastic one-gallon milk jugs, which I might even neglect to rinse. Why would I do such a thing? To prove a point that the best wines are Sonoma wines (and to poison my enemies.)

Of course, Ohio's bustling wine industry has all but evaporated. They probably import more wine from, say, Uruguay – like, one case – than presently produced in the entire state. You might ask, "En Uruguay hay buen vino?" The reply, at least according to the Uruguayan Wine Guide, is "Increíble!" What does this mean? We may never know, however, I know implicitly that Uruguayan wine is vastly superior to whatever might be moldering in some mid-western cellar, which is not a cellar as we might know it but a musty basement that reeks of two-stroke oil and laundry products. I know because I've been there, or least I've flown over it whilst sipping a single-serve bottle of

Sutter Home intended for the palate populi and still felt a justifiable airborne arrogance over Ohio wine, even after I dropped a peanut in my plastic cup (full disclosure, the wine juggernaut is a client.)

"The smallness of the district limits the supply," the ad continues. That statement has less to do with supply and demand than it does with containing a threat to the public. Any larger and then-Gov. John W. Bricker would have been morally obligated to declare a state of emergency. I'm surprised they haven't erected a memorial on the banks of Lake Erie to commemorate the taste buds lost when bottles began shipping from their Wine Grape Paradise. I may not be up on my biblical studies but it seems to me that whenever something leaves paradise it's been exiled because it affronted the natural order.

The ancient *LIFE* advert also boasts that its purchaser, E&K Ohio Wines, has "America's only woman wine steward, Josephine Molera" who "deems it's a privilege to recommend E&K Ohio Wines!" Sadly, 70 years ago, they probably thought it was a privilege for her to have a job at all. Wine, however, has long been a refuge for women, who have made historic inroads into the industry since the 19th century. Now, according to the Wine Institute, women represent about 20 percent of the industry. Presently in Ohio, there's one woman winemaker – Kelly Harvey of Signature Wines, "a boutique, urban micro-winery located in Columbus, Ohio." Yep, there's one lone Buckeye chick making wine in a place where it not only snows but her state's official beverage is tomato juice. And Sonoma's wineries thought they had it tough with a sagging economy, depressed tourism, and schizophrenic weather. It could be worse; you could be a minority in your industry in a rustbelt state where ordering a Virgin Bloody Mary would likely result in public shaming.

Perhaps I should be more circumspect – in another 70 years, some cad writer might pull up this article on his data device du jour and have a haughty laugh about the erstwhile Sonoma wine industry and the hubris with which we celebrated it, you know, before the ice caps melted and our Wine Grape Paradise became an underwater theme-park. Times will change. Until then, we can only try to save it in a bottle.

CIA Operative

Until recently, I'd never been to St. Helena's Wine Spectator Greystone Restaurant. Were it not for a fortuitous luncheon with a client this week, I might never have learned that the Napa County institution is serving up more than my petite hanger steak with glazed yellow wax beans, toybox cherry tomatoes, pancetta, crumbled gorgonzola, and cabernet jus. It's got a cauldron of doom simmering on the back burner, ready to serve to Sonoma.

Tucked into the northerly wing of the Culinary Institute of America, tomorrow's chefs are gaining their gustatory gravitas alongside the best of the Napa Valley and beyond. Let one's mind wander for a moment, however, and it's not hard to imagine Greystone as the Hogwarts of haute cuisine, where dark culinary arts are transferred from one generation to the next. Even the building's name is suggestive of the sort of staid structure one might find in Langley, Va., crossed with the X-Men's school for Mutant Teenagers. And a spice rack.

The fact that Greystone is part of the Culinary Institute of America, or more precisely – CIA – only adds to the impression that, to them, the difference between saucier and super-spy is academic. Literally. Greystone is a school for secret agents camouflaged in toques. The evidence is obvious. The on-campus restaurant is a mere typo away from having the word "spectre" in its name. Need I remind you that SPECTRE stands for "SPecial Executive for Counter-intelligence, Terrorism, Revenge, and Extortion," the very agency that's been trying to kill James Bond all these years?

Consider this: Uber-chef Julia Child's supposition that one's first lesson in the kitchen should be "how to use a knife" takes on new meaning when one considers she was a member of the Office of Strategic Services, a forerunner to the Central Intelligence Agency (one can imagine the CIA uses such instruments for more than deveining shrimp.) Need I say more?

Prior to meeting my wife, my kitchen drawers consisted of little more than a Swiss Army knife. My culinary weaponry has since grown into a full-blown arsenal, however, I've had little occasion to purchase any throwing stars or blow-darts – standard equipment in Napa, I suspect. I wouldn't be able to find such tools of death in Sonoma anyway. If you want to raise eyebrows at the Sign of the Bear Kitchenware, go ahead and ask for throwing stars. A search online at our namesake corporate kitchen store, Williams-Sonoma, yielded only "star anise" and "Star Wars Pancake Molds," which could be considered lethal, at least to one's love life – if you're male, single and own some.

That said, I suspect one might find all manner of stainless steel pokies from any kitchen store in Napa. They're that serious. Why else would they stock *Food and Wine* and *Soldier of Fortune* magazines side by side in those places? *Mastering the Art of French Cooking* sharing a shelf with *Cooking to Kill: The Poison Cookbook* by Ebenezer Murgatroyd? Puh-lease.

And this, methinks, is the primary difference between Napa and Sonoma on the dual fronts of wine and epicurea. Sonomans are satisfied with wine country living as is. Napa won't be satisfied until it achieves world domination (and the perfect soufflé.) Thusly, we must be vigilant, Sonoma. We must discipline our minds, bodies, and palates so that we too are lean, mean, gourmet machines.

To wit, our local culinary school, Ramekins, might consider including a hand-to-hand combat course with its "chewy gooey, crispy crunchy cookie" class. Chewy gooey can only get you so far but an organic, herbal pepper-spray class – now that's cooking with gas. I mean, what are we going to do when the ninjas come? You know what Napa does? They go to Sonoma because they ARE the ninjas. They're coming. We'll be ready. Napa can eat our lunch but we'll take it to breakfast – if you know what I mean.

LonelyRoad116

A few weeks ago, I hooked that right off Stage Gulch Road onto Hwy. 116 and was promptly greeted by one of those gigantic Lite-Brite signs surely telling me something important about the road ahead. I'm a fast driver and a slow reader so I typically catch little of such roadside missives.

What did catch my eye, however, was the tell-tale @ sign – sometimes whimsically known as a "monkey tail" – and associated, universally, with forms of online communication, from email to social networks. One illegal u-turn later and I was able to confirm that Hwy. 116, indeed, has a Twitter account: @sonoma116.

Initially, I thought the notion was absurd seeing as much of Twitter's user-generated messages are often comprised of little more than the ingredients of sandwiches and what cute antic someone's cats just performed.

Since Hwy 116 lacks a roadside deli and the cats that call the highway home usually don't do so for long, I figured I was safe when I later went online to investigate the highway's foray into Web 2.0.

At present writing, @Sonoma116 just tweeted, "Traffic will be reduced to 1 lane from 7 pm to 5 am Tuesday 6/29 through Friday morning 7/2. There will be no closures July 4th weekend."

Good to know – useful information shared with

concision and focus (unlike, say, this column.) Of course, Twitter's 140 character limit helps keep the messages well-pruned, all the better to read while driving, I suppose.

A *Car and Driver* magazine study found that their legally intoxicated test driver took 4 feet of breaking when reacting to a red light. When texting, the amount of feet it took the driver to break was 70. Since Tweeting is really just texting with a cute ornithological nickname, it goes to show that friends don't let friends Tweet and drive.

As it turns out, many thoroughfares have Twitter accounts with varying degrees of usefulness. The Parisians, however, might rue the fact that the "ChampsElysees" is held by someone named Yen Ng who has "protected their tweets" rendering them inaccessible to the general public. Mercifully, one can still "Follow" the "Yellow Brick Road" for updates from Oz. "PetalumaBlvd" is still up for grabs if anyone has a hankering to give voice to P-Town's main artery at 140 characters per tweet. Tweet one: "I'm standing in the intersection where they shot *American Graffiti*." Tweet two: "I'm now in the emergency room."

Because Sonoma's main drag, Broadway, shares its name with the Great White Way, that Twitter account was sewn up years ago – specifically, three years ago with the initial Tweet, "Goin to the show." That tweet was followed up two years later with a query about which Broadway stars are using Twitter. There has been no activity since, though, inexplicably, "Broadway" has 150 followers. Why would 150 people care about the incredibly laconic "Broadway?" Perhaps they have a betting pool as to when it might next tweet. My money's on Never.

Likewise, "VanNess," on of San Francisco's iconic streets, is also lax in the update department. Two years ago, the account holder was "warming up before a gig in North Beach," you know, before going suddenly silent and never tweeting again. One can only imagine the gig didn't go so well. It's neighbor Lombard tweets in Japanese and also went mysteriously mum over a year ago.

The Highway 116 tweets, however, continue thanks to the vigilance of CalTrans' Traci Ruth. When asked what it's like giving voice to a highway she laughed and said "I never really thought of it in that manner" then added that Twitter has become a "vital tool in reaching the public" particularly, she says, along commuter routes where congestion can sometimes be avoided by an informed public choosing alternative routes.

I was sold. I'm now one of Highway 116's 153 "followers." Interestingly, the highway itself is only following one other Twitter profile, that of Highway 101, known on Twitter as "Sonoma101," which sounds more like a sociology class than a highway. At present writing, the Redwood Highway has 162 followers but follows none. It's what I suppose they call a "lonely road."

LonelyRoad, incidentally, has 13 followers and is following 10.

Breakfast of Champions

There are two ways to conduct early a.m. drinking in Sonoma: start the party late and keep going until it's early again; or rise before the sun and scamper down to one of several local taverns, where early birds are always sure to get the tequila worm.

Breakfast of Champions. The phrase, of course, is borrowed from the slogan of Wheaties breakfast cereal, which author Kurt Vonnegut later famously used as the title of his darkly comic novel to the chagrin of the people at General Mills. In the book, Vonnegut included a brief scene in which a cheeky waitress uttered the line every time she served a martini. Thanks to Vonnegut's apt twist, the term has become shorthand for early morning imbibing, not unlike the ubiquitous "hair of the dog," but sans the suggestion of remedy.

To some, the B.O.C. is a lifestyle choice; to others it betokens affliction – but that depends on which side of the bar one falls (literally.) For my editor, the notion had long been an assignment just waiting be written, photographed, and filed (it was either this or some *Candid Camera*-esque article that involved strapping a decoy baby car seat on top of a car). To wit, last week, he dispatched ace shooter Ryan Lely and myself on a reconnaissance mission to suss Sonoma's early-morning drinking scene. The recon mission, however, soon devolved into a "search and destroy" campaign on our livers. Make that Lely's liver, seeing as mine's already a public service announcement in the works. Fortunately, the kid was willing to share.

Our alcoholic odyssey began, as many do, at the office. There, I found Lely at 6 a.m., bright-eyed and checking his email. Lely is a quick-witted, youthful-looking gent in his late-mid-twenties or early-late-twenties depending on how full your philosophical glass is. As he put it "astrologically" he's at the time in life when "Saturn returns." I'm in my early-mid-thirties, which I suppose means Saturn has already come and gone.

We parsed this ancient wisdom bellied to the bar of the Blue Moon Saloon over Bloody Marys. He got carded – I did not. It was 6:11 a.m. and the bar was already serving a handful of regulars. Lely and I briefly fretted how to make contact without sounding like patronizing schmucks. His solution? Loudly comment about how shiny the floor was.

Tense silence.

I braced myself and thought "Good thing the floor is clean, for soon we will be eating it."

Suddenly, a gruff voice barked: "Finally, somebody finally appreciates my goddamn floor!"

This, we learned, was Bill Draeger, a Blue Moon employee, who had indeed polished the bar floor to a shine worthy of Narcissus' reflection.

Draeger, a retiree who volunteers with veterans groups and local historical societies, landed the job by default.

"My friend got sick and said 'Come on in and help me out for a couple weeks,' then he turned around and he died. I wound up with the job permanently. It works out nice – I'm retired, I get up early in the morning. If I stayed in bed until ten o'clock I'd get nothing done. It's something to do," says Draeger. "My day starts at 3:30 a.m., I come clean up the bar before anybody gets here. We get a good crowd here – real nice people."

Indeed, they were nice people and bid us pleasant adieus as we trod to our next destination, careful not to scuff the linoleum.

Steiner's Tavern runs an "early bird" special from 6 to 10 a.m. wherein drinks (specifically of a "non-fancy" variety) can be had for $2.50. Lely ordered a screwdriver and I ordered its cousin, a Greyhound, which, as I explained to the blank-faced bartender, is grapefruit juice and vodka.

"No fancy drinks in the early shift. I don't even have ladies here," the man smiled back as he mixed my drink. "No martinis – no nothing. People just come in and have coffee and brandy, screwdrivers and Bloody Marys sometimes on Sundays."

The atmosphere was convivial and by our second round I thought I'd play the reporter a bit (Lely had already knocked out a few wallet-worthy shots of a patron's canine companion.) I queried the gentleman to my left about his morning ritual and he explained it thusly:

"I usually pick up bread for the café up the street early in the morning, then I come in mostly for the sociability with these guys. It's a group I usually sit with. I always have my drink on the light side so it takes two of them to be one," explained Craig Brown, a youthful, straight-talking 70 year-old. "I'm not here to get drunk, just to socialize – it's the old-timers."

Across the Plaza at the Town Hall, a completely different morning scene transpired. In stark contrast to the collegial attitude of the last joint, the Town Hall had a monastery-like quietude. Its patrons, likewise, seemed focused in a kind of group prayer, but individually, as if the house mantra was "alone, together." There, personal space was premium, privacy paramount and viewer discretion certainly advised. Not that anyone was peering through the bottom of their tumblers into the bar back mirror with the slightest modicum of shame; but it was clear that they would rather not be bothered by a couple of junior varsity barflies with a yen to put their name in the paper. Our $4 bloody marys went quick.

Sufficiently vibed, we scurried back to the west side of the Plaza to the Sunflower Caffe and ordered mimosas.

Unfortunately, it was discovered late that their champagne reserves had run dry so we switched to wine – white wine, which Lely thought would pair better with our waffles. He had 2003 Sonoma County Murphy-Goode chardonnay and I tried the 2003 Deerfield Ranch sauvignon blanc (Lely's was better.)

Having noshed, we were back on our quest for mimosas and soon found ourselves at the Inn at Sonoma on Broadway. How we managed this feat of travel intra-city was lost with the brain cells that fizzled like the sparkling wine poured into our mimosas in the hotel bar.

"I like to make them special," said bartender Mark Watson as he foraged for some strawberries to float atop the drinks.

We retired to a table near the outdoor pool, drank and talked shop with my writing assistant Stacy Stranzl, who moonlights at the Inn as a server. With her keen mind for story, Stranzl quickly assessed that mine and Lely's would end in tragedy if we weren't properly escorted back to the square. Within minutes, we found ourselves riding the complimentary shuttle back to the square as the driver told a tale about having once discovering a drunk in the back of the van at the end of a shift. Lely shot me a suspicious look, but I assured him it wasn't me, I mean, so far as I could remember.

We decided that drink number seven should be a beer – a bracing, punchy beer of the ilk served at Wine Exchange, which we were happy to find opens at 10 a.m. No sooner were the Russian River Blind Pig IPAs poured than we were joined by two haggard young men who had wandered into the bar – one shirtless.

"Our people," I said to Lely, who readied his camera.

These wild-eyed characters revealed themselves to be Australians loosed from a bachelor party that had begun in Las Vegas two days prior. We shared the kind of instant bonhomie that comes naturally to travelers and boozers alike and chatted about our respective drinking traditions.

"It's part of Australian culture. We love to drink our piss early in the day," said Geoff Cobar, invoking Aussie slang for booze. "We've been to Vegas for a 48 hour stay so we're on bit of roll, so we thought we would just keep it going."

Lely and I likewise thought we would continue our Sisyphean roll into alcoholism despite the fact that we had overspent our allotted expense budget by at least twice (I blamed the waffles.)

We staggered to the Girl and the Fig, where coquettish barmaid Sharon Nalezny smiled slyly and concocted for us a witch's brew of Grey Goose vodka, Kaluha, Bailey's Irish Cream, coffee, and whipped cream.

"Oh, my God," Lely appraised.

"We call it the bright-eyed and bushy-tailed," Nalezny wryly replied.

We drank. And drank. We had photos taken of ourselves like belligerent tourists and glad-handedly regaled passersby with tales of our besotted adventure. About twenty minutes and one lethally tasty mojito later (Lely smartly declined this final gambit, still drinking his bright-eyed and bushy-tailed, which had congealed into a kind of alcoholic molasses), I was inexplicably speaking in an Irish accent.

"Holy shit, man, are you feeling it, mate?" I asked in my new-found brogue.

"I'm feeling it. I think we're on par there," Lely answered, stiffening in his seat so as to counter the appearance of being a slovenly drunk.

"What have we learned today, Lely?" I brayed into my recorder. "What on God's earth have we learned?"

"I've learned that drinking early in the morning kind of grays the whole scale, if you will," said Lely.

I nodded and pretended to understand what he meant. He continued: "I think we're both doing a good job being upstanding citizens of humanity."

"Of the world! Drunks are citizens of the world!" I

countered.

"Anyone who met us on the street – we would wax poetic with them for a while and they wouldn't understand what was happening, but still enjoy it in the process."

"Moreover, they would enjoy us."

"Oh, they would definitely enjoy us," Lely agreed.

For a moment, it seemed the room was finally spinning in synch with the turn of the globe – which is to say at about 1000 miles an hour.

Lely and I connected glasses in what we both knew was the last toast of the day. We agreed it was time to head back to the office to prove to Omarzu that his plot to kill us with kindness and booze had failed – you know why? You know why? I'll tell you why...

In the motion picture version of this binge, the scene fades out on the sentimental notes of Queen's "We Are the Champions," because my friend, we are the champions of the world...That's why.

To Boldly Clo Where No Man Has Clo'd Before

She's everywhere in Wine Country – if it weren't for all the vineyards, one might think we lived in one vast dairy farm lorded over by a cartoon cow with a propensity for milk-themed puns.

The iconic Clo the Cow made her billboard debut in1969 and later began her award-winning reign of puns thanks to the creative minds at Benefield, Levinger, McEndy & Vernon, a Santa Rosa-based ad agency now known as VeVa Communications.

Since its inception, the campaign has remained essentially the same – the great two-dimensional head of Clo the Cow grins vacantly toward the roadside, gussied in some order of cultural meme, humorously explicated by wordplay. A vivid illustration of the Clo concept and its relative malleability is the "Mooona Lisa" billboard that featured the cow as Da Vinci's famed "Mona Lisa," in the most successful parody of the painting since Duchamp painted a mustache on her. Later, following the popularity of Dan Brown's the "Da Vinci Code" she appeared in Da Vinci's "Last Supper" as "The Da Vinci Clo."

Of course, not all of Clo's guises have been hits. In 1993, the campaign had a legal confrontation with television aquanaut Jacques Cousteau for its "Jacques Cowsteau" billboard. (The case was dropped when the Frenchman determined the punning bovine was an homage rather than an affront.) Likewise, not all of Clo's iterations spring from the minds of VeVa Communications. Twenty years ago, Clover Stonetta prevailed upon the public for pun-laden aphorisms befitting their beloved bovine in a popular billboard contest. Over 7,000 entries were submitted and many went on to become billboards, including that year's winner "Tip Clo through your two lips."

Now, Clover Stornetta is reprising the contest. As the press release reads, "Clover Stornetta Farms is celebrating the 20th anniversary of the last Clover billboard contest. We want your billboard ideas! If you get a kick out of Clo the Cow and her outrageous puns, now is your chance to see your own ideas come to life on one of our novel billboards."

Oh, man, that's just asking for it – not to mention the $5,000 first prize and inclusion in "Wholly Cow II," the second published anthology of the campaign.

Near the time of the original contest, my gang and I were publishing a satire tabloid entitled SCAM Magazine and being snarky young men with rather juvenile senses of humor, we thought we would go Clo the Cow-tipping and publish our own interpretation of the campaign.

Our minds newly infected by a junior college critical theory class, we decided we couldn't abide the Orwellian ubiquity of Clover Stornetta's marketing throughout "Sonoma Cownty." Mind you, this is back in those precious years when young men are prone to calling any kind of perceived authority (parents, teachers, cartoon cows) as "fascist." To wit, our grand idea was to depict Clo the Cow as a dictator. The resultant effort included depictions of "Fidel Cowstro," "Cao Tse-Tung," "Clo-Chi Minh" and, my favorite, "Moossolini."

Now, mind you, I have no grudge against Clover

Stornetta Farms, the three-generation family-owned and -operated dairy located in my native city of Petaluma, but I'll admit to chewing the cud of satire whenever it seems warranted. Now it's your turn. Clover Stornetta is receiving billboard ideas through October 31. To submit, go to www.cloverstornetta.com, and click on the "Online Contest" tab. Contestants can also visit Clover Stornetta's Facebook page (of course!) at www.facebook.com/cloverstornetta.com and follow the link. And if your dairy drollery isn't cheesy enough, take my advice, don't cry over spilt milk.

Newspaperman

People frequently ask "How do you like working at the *Sonoma Index-Tribune*?" Though I'm flattered they think I'm worthy of the 130-something institution, it's patently untrue. I'm neither worthy nor work there. Sure, I toss a few hundred words over the transom every week, but I'm seldom allowed in the building. The only time I'm invited in is when a suspicious package arrives for me from Vineburg and they want me to hand it to the bomb squad.

I am a mere columnist, or more broadly, a "contributor" though I anticipate that in some post-junta future, a military tribunal might someday declare me a "collaborator." That'll be a proud march to the gallows. As they slip the nooses around our necks, I'll look to my fellow collaborators and quip, "J.M., look good in a tie," and he'll say, "So that's what 'gallows humor' means? I thought it was a band we opened for in the 80s!" and we'll all laugh until some wag groans, "Hang in there" but it will be too late to kick their ass.

Until then, it's a privilege to pen weekly columns for this paper of record and contribute, in some small way, to the timeline of the Sonoma Valley. Years from now, future historians may data-mine some cloud-based neuro-storage archival device and read these very words. What will they discover besides my long-forgotten genius? Perhaps they will find the dawning consciousness that will define their era; or perhaps the seedlings of a cultural renaissance that will inspire generations. Or a typo. Odds are, only one will prove correct and I'm hesitant to prognosticate about the *future* for fear of being… right.

As regular readers can attest, this column has often served as a whiteboard of sorts for its author. Here, I'm granted the opportunity to experiment, cogitate, and commit within the relatively safe confines of our small town, before flouncing out and embarrassing myself on the world stage. You, darling readers, are the beta test, the 1.0, the early adopters – in short, the Guinea pigs. Don't take offense – in some countries you're a delicacy. In time, Sonoma's epicurea scene will catch up with these exotic locales, and we too will eat Guinea pig and think fondly of you. Yes, you put the "Mmm" in "Hmm," which is better than putting the "uh" in "duh" or putting your money into real estate anywhere near the west side.

What's interesting about being a small-town columnist is that readers will often take the time to share their observations about one's work when recognized. Such is the utility of the mug-shot, which also serves those who wish to avoid me. Due to the fact that my name is unpronounceable outside of Ancient Greece, people frequently hear Daedalus Howell (pronounced "DAY-de-lus Howl") when introduced as "David LaSalle." Prior to my mug running with the column, I'd spend entire dinner parties chatting with people as Mr. LaSalle until someone said, "You know who I can't stand reading is that egomaniac in the *I-T*." I'll say, "You mean J.M.?" and they'd reply, "No, the narcissus who only writes about himself" and I'd realized they confused their Greek gods and explain, "I actually pronounced it 'the Daedalus.'" Dessert would be served in silence until I pointed out that "I don't write about myself; I write about Sonoma – I just happen to be in it." Then I'd be asked to leave without even having to help with the dishes. So, you see, I don't work for the paper – it works for me.

Friendly neighborhood Sonoma-Man

Superheroes have long cloaked themselves in the inky vestments of media – what better way for Superman and Spider-Man to moonlight? Their respective gigs as reporter Clark Kent and photographer Peter Parker keep them in the field where they're available to deter dastardly deeds, vanquish villains and keep the karmic balance of metropoleis the world over. If the superheroes aren't keeping media day-jobs, their girlfriends are – Batman could always count on his main squeeze, Vicky Vale, to get the gossip to Gotham. If Superman missed a deadline, Lois Lane always had the straight dope. Superheroes and media are like chocolate and peanut butter – or, as we say in Sonoma – prosciutto and melon.

Given the surfeit of media in our small town, it's a wonder that Sonoma hasn't revealed itself to be a haven for superheroes (It's of note that crime-fighting comic strip heroine-reporter Brenda Starr was hatched by Dale Messick, who lived her final years but ten miles down the highway.) Odds are that one or more of our fine media mavens boasts some order of secret identity and has used it for the common good (though the notion of music columnist James Marshall Berry in tights might technically be an act of evil-doing.)

The Image of the Journalist in Popular Culture, a database containing "conflicting images of the journalist in film, television, radio, fiction, commercials, cartoons, comic books, music, art," currently features 357 references to the query "superhero." Run by the Norman Lear Center at University of Southern California, Annenberg, the online resource is overseen by scholar Joe Saltzman who recently opined in an interview:

"A reporter is an obvious disguise for a superhero because it puts the superhero right in the thick of the news and gives him or her an opportunity to know what is going on in the city, the country, and the world… It is no surprise that the most enduring image of the journalist is the *Daily Planet* family – Clark Kent (Superman), Lois Lane, Perry White and Jimmy Olsen."

It's a gratifying sentiment for sure, which, for me, leads inevitably to the notion of which super-personae my colleagues might portray. With the risk of inadvertently outing one or more of their alter-egos, I won't task-the-mask with spurious speculation but rather envision what superheroes Sonoma needs to remedy its particular evils.

For example, The Spork, also known as the Culinary Conundrum, might just be the avenging angel of local comestibles. It's not uncommon that a guileless gastronome must be rescued from the evils of "epidrearia," when local foodstuffs aren't up to snuff. Moreover, the Spork must avenge Vinoman, who was offed by the evil Stain, a once mild-mannered wine writer who transforms into a burgundy-hued hellion when he imbibes his secret elixir – cheap wine. Stain is also in the sights of the Prophet of Non, whose beat is Sonoma's ubiquitous non-profit industry by day and punishing tax improprieties at night (you know who you are!) Of course, "dotting the eyes and crossing the tease" throughout is the Sonoma Editrix, who would just as soon cut your nut-graf as polish your news-peg.

There's more, surely, lurking behind a copy-desk, a microphone, a camera lens – all ready to don the cape and take on the machinations of the Historic Sonoma Plasma and other scourges to our fair burg. What's germane is that these pursuers of truth, justice and the American way, no matter their affiliation, no matter their media, are all superheroes in their own right. They've committed their lives to telling the greatest story of all – our story.

Roadside Attraction

There are few invitations to adventure more alluring than a diamond-shaped orange road sign inscribed in sans-serif font. For us workaday chaps for whom the morning commute represents the pinnacle of one's quotidian exposure to danger and intrigue, it hardly matters what's written on the sign. Of course, "Falling Rocks" has a little more implicit danger than "Soft shoulder," though the latter certainly compensates with its flicker of intrigue. By far the most interesting signs are the ones that read "Detour," since they interrupt our well-established patterns and force us to act – albeit, often by merely turning left – but who knows what lays beyond? I certainly didn't.

Since the real estate market exiled me to the Springs, I've forgotten the "nuisance of nuance" that is Sonoma's road plan – or as often, the seeming lack of it. I no longer distinguish between East and West; my mental map of Sonoma simply consists of "here" and "there." And "there" can be a relative labyrinth when you throw in a detour sign or two.

One would think that a guy named Daedalus would have a handle on labyrinths, seeing as the name comes from the mythological Greek character said to have invented the notion (in his case, to contain the Minotaur and sundry other mythic miscreants.) Not I, at least not when it came to navigating the detour set up on Fifth Street West this week. This is in no way a criticism of the fine people who performed the open-heart surgery on the artery between Fifth Street West and West Spain last week, in particular, the stretch of street bisected by the bike path. Of the two main arteries to and from the Springs, this is my preferred route, not least of which because its rectilinear pathway usually adheres to a predictable grid (the sweeping arc of Hwy. 12 that splinters into Riverside Drive has always made me nervous, in part because of the sign on the landscaped island dividing the road which reads "Xeriscape," a word which looks like space-alien lingo for "We're buried here.")

When either Fifth Street West or any length of Hwy. 12 is closed for more than a couple of minutes, chaos ensues. Unless, of course, there's a "Detour" sign – though in my case, it should be footnoted with the disclaimer "Hope you packed a lunch because you will be driving in circles for the next half an hour."

It's my own fault. I drive like a lemming. I merely followed the car in front of me, who in turn, was following the car in front of them, which was apparently driven by a blind person. This is too bad because there are many sights worth seeing when traveling down Lasuen Drive, where our detour began. For example, I'd never seen Grace Baptist Church Fellowship Hall before and its signage regarding the "New Wine Fellowship." I'm assuming they don't have a tasting room but can testify that I've "seen the light" refracted through a wine glass on a few occasions and am happy to know they're there.

Our lost caravan didn't stop at Grace, or our other geographic discovery, Olsen Park. We sallied forth, the blind leading the blind, up Juaquin Drive where we spied another band of detoured motorists circling Sherman Court, unaware that they were following their own tail, so to speak. As we watched them turning in this existential gyre, our collective instinct to help redirect them was waylaid by the mutual assessment that they'd just slow up our own escape. So we left them to perish.

Ay, if only we had shown some compassion. Our karma was served up soon enough when we found ourselves trapped in the cul de sac that caps Mitchell Way, unable to re-enter the stream of cars heading toward freedom. The other drivers had likely witnessed our callous forsaking of the Sherman Court Convoy (may they rest in peace) and proceeded to block we Mitchell Way Wanderers from entering the flow of traffic.

It is from there that I write you now, dear readers. Please, for the love of God, show some mercy. Or at least, the way to Linda Drive.

F'queue: The Art of Waiting in Line in Sonoma

It used to be Napa and Marin – counties historically assailed for propagating cultures of entitlement, privilege and general snobbery – that bred expectations of social superiority among the chattering classes. Turns out, there's a homemade breed, which, to the awesome chagrin of a score of patrons El Dorado Kitchenette one recent morning, made itself woefully apparent.

A middle-aged woman juggling a cell phone, a half-hearted conversation with some sister-in-arms and an order that could caffeinate an infantry, managed to not only change her order twice in mid-stream (swapping muffins for cinnamon rolls and back again due to the apparently offensive discovery of raisins), she single-handedly stalled the queue such that it swelled out the door as a beleaguered staff swarmed and tried vainly to accommodate ever-changing whims.

Even the village weirdo rolled his eyes (you know who you are) as the woman continued her endless order. And the baristas! Those poor, bedraggled young people – heroes, really – who sallied forth, smiles embroidered upon faces once aglow with youth and the possibilities of life, washed away by this upper-middleclass sea serpent having a slash from upstream the economic estuary.

The man behind me opened his balled fist to sweep

away the sweat accruing on his brow as he muttered something about justifiable homicide. The parking police, who otherwise could have cleaned up while we waited past our two-hour allotments, eased their vigilance from empathy.

Clocks died.

A montage of calendar pages blown by the Winds of Time fell to the floor in heaps of temporal torpor. The estate of Jean Paul Sartre considered suing for what appeared an unauthorized staging of "No Exit." Reflecting on the patience of Job was a momentary comfort until we realized he'd probably have renounced God and popped off to 7-11 for a flavored coffee an eon earlier.

And still, this awful Sonoman (yes, sadly, a Sonoman) would not quit.

Were she simply oblivious, we could at least marvel at her self-absorption – a perfect feed-loop of reflection and exaltation at the exaltation of her reflection; the "mirror, mirror" on the wall slipped atop a photocopier, a video camera pointed at the TV. At some point, the snake eating its own tail must also eat its own crap, right? Theoretically, yes, but only after eating all the pastries at EDK.

Those of us (still) in line were shocked, having only witnessed such abhorrent, selfish behavior in comic portrayals of our neighbors to the East and South – and those, I realized, were exaggerated. This woman's attitude was neither Napanese or Marinite – it was some vile hybrid, some hellish affliction likely born of Nazi science.

And this I learned: The customer is not always right. Sometimes the customer is so bloody wrong that the rest of us can only look on in dumbfounded fury, paralyzed by useless etiquette and the sinking feeling that our species has camouflaged its devolution with mobile phones and trips to the outlet mall. Survival of the specious.

I suppose moments like this are like watching zoo animals mate in captivity. It's simultaneously comic and alarming when beasts enact the will of nature, which, naturally, highlights our own clumsy attempts to distinguish ourselves as something other than selfish animals. Of course, we can't all be bonobos, though that would certainly make the coffee line at EDK more interesting and, in some cases, faster. We can only stand erect (that's "upright" you filthy buggers), groping up the food chain toward the civil transaction of brown water from one primate to another. That is, if there is any left.

Stave Off

Barrel staves get used for all sorts of objects d'art. Candleholders, planter boxes, artificial bow legs. But an ark? Given the deluge of rain in recent weeks, wineries will soon have no choice but to prepare for a flood of biblical proportions. And by way of analogy to their Old Testament predecessor, they will be forced to choose which of their wines they will bring with them.

Biblical scholars might argue that, like Noah, winemakers should bring all of their wines just as the ur-zookeeper is alleged to have brought all the animals. He didn't. I contend some animals were left behind. Ever hear of the pygmy maunderaffe? Yep, selected out by Noah. Or perhaps eaten mid-journey. The point is, it's gone and similar sacrifices will also have to be made as the Great Flood of Sonoma looms.

How do vintners choose which wines to bring with them to our brave new and wet world? Believe me, at some point analysis paralysis will kick in. In *The Paradox of Choice: Why More is Less*, author Barry Schwartz observes "Our evaluation of our choices is profoundly affected by what we compare them with, including comparison with alternatives that exist only in our imaginations."

Okay. Here's where I can help you. I just so happen to be an expert at divining real wines from those that may be imaginary. I'm blessed with a palate that can tell the difference by merely sampling the wines in question (I know, it's amazing.) At the very least I can aid in eliminating some of the guesswork. Eliminating the excess wine deemed unsuitable for your ark is another matter entirely. Fortunately, this also falls within the area of my expertise. Rarely have the words "excess" and "wine" been so perfectly represented in one man. I am that man.

The most effective means of permanently removing wine from a cellar is drinking it. For many, this may seem a daunting task – so many bottles, so little geological time. Fortunately, I lead a crack team of seasoned cellar drainers who are at the ready to ease your transition into Water World. In fact, given the enormity of the crisis upon us, I will waive our usual fee. Why would I do that? Because, Sonoma, I care. I care about our heritage as California's first wine growing region, I care about our award-winning wines and our provenance in an industry that is the raison d'etre for much of what defines the valley. I'd be damned to see that legacy destroyed, when all it takes to save it is popping a few corks and some rented Reidel stemware. You may call it sacrifice but I call it community. We're here for you, Sonoma. And your wine. Particularly the 2005 and 2007 vintages.

Remember, when traveling the roiling seas, it's always prudent to travel light – you've got to float, right? Therefore, I recommend only bringing a few, select bottles aboard your ark. We all know about ships in bottles – trust me, it doesn't work the other way around. "Bottles in ships" just doesn't sound right, especially during these soggy end days. And while you're trying to puzzle out what the hell I'm talking about, consider that another 10 million raindrops just fell. Think about it. Time is running out and you can't save it in a bottle, so you should probably just let us get to work.

Perhaps someday, future generations may look back on these antediluvian days and remember a few hardy souls doing their best to preserve the future of your wine by drinking its past, as we're swept away, clinging to a barrel stave adrift on the wine-dark sea.

We're Number Two!

My email inbox is a magnet for publicity spam, particularly those breathless missives regarding the "wine country experience." How can I tell the difference between spam and a press release in the nanosecond before I delete it? If it's about Napa, it's spam. Seeing as my beat is decidedly Sonoman, I haven't the time or inclination to study up on the "other" wine country. Except when the headline crows from the subject line "Napa Valley Honored as the World's Top Food & Wine Destination."

Cue the sad trombone.

Apparently, TripAdvisor, the online travel site, which encourages its users to "Find Deals, Read Reviews from Real People. Get the Truth. Then Go," held an opinion poll as part of its 2010 TripAdvisor Traveler's Choice Destination Awards and from "millions of real reviews and opinions that actual travelers share with each other on the popular travel website" concluded that Napa Valley was tops.

The fact that theirs was not a scientific poll notwithstanding, Sonoma should be aware that its neighbor to the east is already mounting its case for the world's tourism dollars – hard, cold cash that could be ours for the taking with just a modicum of moxie.

Bolinas, CA, the coastal West Marin enclave, which

sometimes refers to itself as "The Republic of Bolinas," routinely removes the roadside signage along Hwy 1 that indicates where one might turn to visit it. This ritual rebuff to tourists and developers is legend and has certainly added to Bolinas' mystique, if not helped preserve whatever it is the republic is hiding from the world (dilithium crystals, I bet.)

Now here in Sonoma, we're big on signage. One can't drive down Hwy. 121 into our valley without being besieged by a number of billboards extolling our virtues as "Real Wine County" or asking us not to sit in the big blue chairs in front of Cornerstone. We're too invested in our signs to even consider using Bolinas' reverse-psychology approach to boosting tourism through obscurity. Instead, we should introduce this approach to Napa, by removing their signs.

In order to get to Napa from the Hwy. 101 corridor, one must drive through Sonoma County, whereupon one might see a number of signs directing tourists and their pocket books out of town. Now, I ask you, why would we ever put signs on our own land instructing people how to visit our competition? Have we not deferred enough to Napa? It's as if we're saying, "Welcome to Sonoma, Napa is right this way." Must we remain the overlooked second son? These things never end well, just ask Shakespeare. Invariably, the wine gets poisoned and everybody dies.

How many times have visiting friends called you from the road having missed that crucial turn in Schellville only to find themselves about to hook a left on Hwy. 29 into the heart of Napa? Even if we remove all of Napa's signs, Sonoma still needs bigger signs – Carneros Hwy. should look like the Strip in Vegas, with enough blinking lights to cause epileptic seizures.

Too gaudy? Perhaps we could go conceptual and create a sign that offers directions to either "Heaven" or

"Hell" (despite what the teenagers say, Sonoma would be Heaven). Or, even more abstractly – "Ginger" or "Mary Ann" (Sonoma is Mary Ann, duh). Or, we could just build a wall.

Meanwhile, Clay Gregory, CEO of The Napa Valley Destination Council, gloats from my inbox. "From stunningly beautiful locales to spots with outstanding attractions, the 2010 Travelers' Choice Destination Award winners are truly incredible places that travelers love – and we are honored to be selected as the world's number one Food and Wine Destination."

Which, I guess, is also a way of saying we're number two. We should spam this column to him.

Sprung

"I imagine heaven to be a lot like Spring in Sonoma," said San Francisco Chronicle columnist Herb Caen. He would know – he's dead. For those with allergies, Spring in Sonoma can be a living hell.

At present writing, the pollen count is so high that Weather.com, which tracks this sort of data, is unable to chart it properly – it's beyond "high" on its scale. It's record-setting as well as nose-running, eye-watering, throat-searing and generally miserable-making. Like a bad M. Night Shyamalan movie, seasonal allergies are how plants avenge themselves.

Perhaps we deserve it. Consider the dead Christmas tree on the side of your neighbor's house. Not only do we annually decimate forests of vegetable brethren, we humiliate the resulting corpse with gaudy decorations and bring it final shame by letting it dry into dust in the company of garbage cans. Why else would a brown Christmas tree be visible in May? It's the arboreal equivalent of a head on a spike and it sends a clear signal to the plant world: We will kill you. Oh, and sometimes we eat you too.

What many often fail to realize during this seasonal assault on our noses is that the distribution of pollen is how plants reproduce. Yes, we're in the midst of some kind of herbaceous orgy. Perhaps we're lucky that all we're getting are the sniffles instead some sort of plant-clap. At least plant-clap can be treated with standard antibiotics (or so I hear.) The allergies that attack Sonomans, however, require a battery of pharmaceuticals, (fexofenodrine, pseudoephedrine, etc.), which means your medicine cabinet is a Bunsen burner away from becoming a meth lab. This is what the junkies are looking for when they come in the bathroom window. However, during Spring in Sonoma, it might just be the uninsured seeking decongestant relief.

Despite the enormity of my nose (useful for processing all this hot air), I'm immune to most airborne allergens. My wife, the Contessa, however, is not nor it seems is our son the Cannoli, both of whom sneeze with enough regularity as to suggest a renewable energy source. The difference between green and gesundheit is negligible, especially when pronounced with a stuffy nose.

My tolerance of local pollen notwithstanding, I have noticed a peculiarly Sonoman sensitivity to wine when I've enjoyed it in extremis. After a few bottles, I often awake with a headache, occasional nausea and the rare, but memorable, supplication to the porcelain god as I lay prone upon the cool tile of the bathroom floor. I attribute my proclivity to vomit rather than sneeze to good genes. I pity my poor Roman ancestor who, upon taking a vomitorium break during wine-soaked bacchanal, could only muster a torrent of sneezes. How embarrassing (if he were a tree, he'd surely have been stripped of his leaves and beset by tire swings.)

I once knew a woman who claimed to be allergic to California wines owing to the presence of sulfites. Consequently, she refused anything but pricier French wine. However, there is no such beast as a sulfite-free wine due to the fact that, even when they're not added to eliminate bacteria, sulfites occur naturally during fermentation. The real difference between our wines and those on the continent is that the FDA requires our labels to read "Contains sulfites," whereas Europeans have no such requirements. Now, when our wines, like prescription medicines, are required to list side effects, we will know we've gone too far. "May cause drowsiness," check; "Some dizziness may occur," check; "Do not operate motor vehicles or heavy machinery," double-check. Of course, the active ingredient is nothing to sneeze at either.

Wine, The Original Social Networking

Sure, Facebook may be all the rage for those seeking an online community experience, but wine was and remains the preferred social networking experience for the unplugged, or at least the uncorked, set.

Prior to modern winery practices (and the public health code), making wine was a socially-driven endeavor in which people bared their soles and stomped grapes in barrels. Surely some order of social networking occurred in these cozy bacchanals, if not outright orgies. The DNA of hot tubs and the Jacuzzi can surely be traced to this common ancestor, as well as, I suppose, dozens of families of Mediterranean descent.

In this context, notions of "rubbing elbows," "elbow grease" and "social lubrication" are merely iterations of an evolving network. Though each can stand on its own, as can "being social" and "networking," the notions are more effective when forged together, the way it's understood that rubbing and lubrication benefit from a well-greased elbow.

I recently stumbled into a wine marketing conference due to the machinations of a publicist with a grudge to get as many media-butts in seats as possible, no matter how qualified. For a gratis pour of wine, I'll be anyone's ass. The marketers were concerned with acquainting the so-called X and Y Generations with their product by embracing viral videos, blogs, podcasts, and social networking sites with such zeal that they used the unfortunate term "Wine 2.0."

What they failed to notice was that we're already into wine – some of us since grade school. This, I attribute to Orson Welles.

In late 1970s, a furrow-browed Welles pitched Paul Masson jug wine in TV commercials, famously harrumphing "We shall sell no wine before it's time." I took him seriously. Albeit, Masson's ad men weren't attempting to foment early brand-loyalty with the single-digit set; wine had none of the ersatz sophistication promised by the candy cigarettes peddled by Big Tobacco. Even at age seven, I was sufficiently intrigued by this corpulent Anti-Claus to forge a mental bond between wine and my burgeoning sense of urbanity (a notion temporarily eclipsed, of course, by the advent of the juice box.)

Welles would sell me no wine until it was time, which was about 14 years later when I was of age. However, at 16, given my penchant for blazers and newly infected with a British accent, which had spread through the high school drama club like mono, I was able to bamboozle the employees at the local liquor store. My misdemeanor of choice? Wine. Why, what else, Mr. Welles?

"Do you have ID?" a clerk would ask as my crime wave expanded beyond my small town.

"Me passport's in me luggage, mate," I'd brogue, then smile brightly as if to say "Now, let's not mar this moment of international diplomacy then."

It's only now that I've realized that, as my gang's designated buyer, I was shaping their virgin palates. This could account for the enduring popularity of bottom-shelf product in my home town. In retrospect, I would have been more selective, but a $5 budget is to selectivity as adolescence is to discretion, which is why the legend of my Christ-like ability to turn their liquid assets into wine had spread. Within months, I was supplying most of my town's class of '90 with jugs of California plonk simply labeled "Red."

Despite the fact that even the most technically advanced

of my brood could barely operate the clasp of a girl's bra, I purchased bottles with corks and never screw caps (I ran a classy operation.) This necessitated mastery of such arcane instruments as the Ah So or the lethal-looking, android Jumping Jack otherwise known as a "winged" corkscrew, about which I'd lead impromptu seminars in the shadows of American Alley before trundling off to some poetry reading or other.

I dare say that the girls huddled in the abandoned shack we called our "studios" were little impressed with the poetry we recited, hushed and humid over candlelight – male display behavior muddied by a midsummer night's drunk. More to the point, the girls were there for the wine, not the poets. Only after a couple of champion swigs by both parties could we even hope them to be the least bit susceptible to our charms, especially those in verse. But eventually, we networked.

After much meditation, I believe I've found the wine bar analog to MySpace: The next time you order a wine by the glass, ask your sommelier to acquaint you with the other patrons with whom you are sharing the bottle. Though it may result in a raised eyebrow, it might also garner a friendly smile and if you're lucky, some greasy elbows.

My Big Fat Greek Cooking Show

Several years ago, during the media mania that followed upon the release of indie hit *My Big Fat Greek Wedding*, cable TV producers became aggressive about packaging any show they could with *My Big Fat Greek*-whatever in the title. For the better part of a season, all things Greek were the rage in Hollywood – a Jimmy the Greek biopic was discussed, studios acquired El Greco paintings for their lobbies and instead of lunch, everyone did gyros. This is how I ended up with my own cooking show. For ten minutes.

Owing to the dumb luck of being born to a pair of classics students, I was blessed/cursed with the Greco-Anglo appellation "Daedalus Howell." Some say I fared better than my brother Dartagnan who was born during a French literature seminar. However, Dart's nickname is full of inherent swagger and breezy machismo, whereas mine is most often pronounced as if it should be preceded by Grateful. No matter how it's mispronounced, however, its primary disconnect in my life is that fact that I'm not Greek, or at least no more than any other ostensibly white guy living in 21st century America.

The trunk of my family tree is so obscured by generations of poor records management that I generally skip ahead to its roots such that, after my grandfather, it's all cave dwellers and monkeys. Those ancient paintings in the Chauvet-Pont-d'Arc Cave? Yeah, I'm related to the guy who did those. You probably are too, so I guess we're cousins (this was the very excuse I used to extricate myself from a particularly sticky romantic entanglement.)

I'm told I'm mostly Irish and Cherokee, which, beyond pervasive stereotypes of alcoholism (which I've personally tried to dispel using reverse psychology and an open tab) also means my people have had serious troubles keeping the English-speakers from taking over their nations. This could by why I'm so flagrant about claiming Greece as my country of origin whenever someone asks. I don't care and I can bring an end to the conversation when, after they inevitably say "Opa!" I reply, "We don't really say that. In fact, it's racist."

Now, I've shared this back-story with you because it's essentially the same story I told a producer at a certain network associated with things people put in their mouths. You know the one, it's a four-letter word that starts with F. And it's rated G.

The woman on the opposite side of the desk went red with panic and said in no uncertain terms was I ever to tell anyone I wasn't actually Greek. It suddenly became clear that the only reason I'd gotten in the door was on account of my Greekish name and that no other acceptable candidate had emerged despite a thriving Southern California Greek community. Or more to the point, she had mere days to package the show because she had spent the preceding weeks in rehab. Her assistant covered for her as best she could but now it was down to the wire. She asked, "Do you know what 'plausible deniability' means?"

"It's Greek to me," I quipped. Her eyes narrowed and she said, "That's a great tag line. It's like Larry the Cable Guy's 'Git 'er done!' but without the *Deliverance* vibe." I agreed, then suggested that I could say the line after I made, say, a grilled cheese sandwich (the extend of my culinary prowess at the time), then shrug and say, "It's Greek to me." She frowned so I added "Of course, I'd slather it in tzatziki sauce. She smiled and I thought to myself, I'm in.

All I have to do is tell them what they want to hear and learn everything I can about Greek condiments.

I went home and threw myself into researching all I could about what the Greeks put on their food. Turns out tzatziki is about it, at least according to the first page of Google search results. For a country credited with the invention of Western Civilization, they sure slacked off in the condiment department. I made a mental note to never order a hot dog in Greece. I also realized that My Big Fat Greek Cooking Show was "tha fas xilo" (going to eat wood) unless I developed an angle.

I decided to rip off everything Socrates by contemporizing his more famous quotes with food notions. For example, "the unexamined food is not worth eating." Perfect. Not only could it work for the show, I thought, it will probably become a slogan for health inspectors. "I am the wisest man alive, for I know one thing, and that is that I know nothing...about Greek food." Or for portion control, "He is richest who is content with the least... moussaka." And "Never drink ouzo on an empty stomach." The last one is entirely my own, though I'm sure Socrates would agree.

My next audition was a wash. It wasn't because I hadn't become sufficiently Greek but because the producer's assistant had successfully pitched a show about drug interventions to a sister network and my producer was going to star. Besides, I was told, the Greek trend had peaked and interest was swinging back toward French cuisine.

"Have you met my brother Dartagnan?" I asked.

501s

Given the choice, most days I'd rather write an obituary than a "mission statement." Never will one find a more studiously vague and broadly inclusive stab at presupposing purpose than that slim paragraph that follows the words "Our Mission." I've written a few as a hired gun and shot through others as a reporter. Nasty business either way.

In our town, where everyone seems to run, chair, or benefit by a non-profit, mission statements are de rigeur. After wine and tourism, profitably non-profiting has proven smart business. In fact, there has been speculation that "Sonoma" is the Miwok term for "501(c)(3)."

Those guys are gone now but they'd be proud to know that most of these organizations do tremendous good for our community. It could be argued that many provide the fabric from which our community is woven.

Others, perhaps, make wonderful tax shelters and provide a means to launder filthy lucre into outsized salaries for a crafty few. There's a six-figure salary awaiting the brilliant mind with enough nerve to create a local non-profit watchdog group and milk it all the way to a non-extradition country before the audit kicks in. Check out the filings online sometime, it's a hoot.

Remember the good old days when "501" was preceded by "Levi's." For some Sonomans, to paraphrase Brooke

Shields, nothing comes between them and their 501s. Glad they still fit. Now that tax time is looming, like many, I too have been looking for a fit, namely any write-off within the IRS's narrow (in my opinion) definition of a tax-deductible donation.

I have it on good authority from my CPA that bar tabs don't apply (the amount of "meals and entertainment" deductions make my business seem much more fun than I recall.) Of the few hundred non-profits in town, doesn't one run a pub? I know many a donor ready to give generously to the "Raise a Pint Foundation." Some may give so much that they develop "donating problems," which will lead another non-profit to print bumper-stickers that read "Friends don't let friends donate drunk."

Donating drunk, of course, is a Sonoma tradition. If you've ever given at a fundraising event, a glass or more of wine likely preceded your act of munificence. Not that you've been taken advantage of. Chances are that the market value of the gallons of wine we've imbibed at these functions far exceeds the cash most of us have given. But don't fret – the virtuous circle is completed by the fact that the wine was donated too. Moreover, you're doing the organizers a favor by drinking all the booze, otherwise some hapless volunteer has to lug it all back to HQ where it will be systematically drained over the next few months by interns.

And trust me, there's nothing more dangerous to an organization than a drunk intern, especially when they start yapping to the media about how their boss is a con-man and how they're going to start their own non-profit "scam" when they graduate. If I was on the clock maybe I'd care, but I need the write-off, kiddo, so have another glass and jot down that Tax ID number.

While you're at it, perhaps you should amend your

organization's mission statement. Grab the nearest newspaper, pick an obituary at random and steal the last paragraph. That's where the money is. Frequently these days, they encourage mourners to forgo flowers and instead make a charitable donation in the deceased's name (yeah, florists hate that part). Now, post your improvements on the NPO's website. Granted, the talk of flowers and death won't jibe with the crap about "community" or "outreach" or whatnot, but at least the intentions will read honestly. Then perhaps, intern, you might actually buy the wine from which the truth spills.

With Fond Sediments

As one of Sonoma's resident soothsayers, I'm always on the hunt for a means of prognosticating the future that is both germane to the local experience and vague enough to be projected upon in any way one desires – something between a Rorschach inkblot and poorly drawn tarot card.

I found it. My divining tool of choice comes through a wine glass, darkly. Make that an empty wine glass in which sediments have been left behind. Those crystalline chunks of violet tartrates are secret messages from the future that can be read like tea leaves, the lines of the palm, or the furrows in the brows of one's readers. Of course, interpreting order in chaos or its cousin randomness or its pretty girlfriend chance, has its hazards. This is why I've put together these handy guidelines below.

If you discover you have sediments in your glass, do not reel in terror that you've been drinking purple dirt. You've just been invited to peer into the future. Raise your glass to the light and turn it such that you're looking at from the bottom up (tea leaf readers do the opposite and consequently are always "looking down" on the future, which it hates). Regard how the sediment is distributed in relation to the stem of your wine glass. If you're not drinking your wine from a wine glass, you may position a pencil at the bottom of your mayonnaise jar or whatever you're using to achieve the same effect.

Now, notice how the sediment is concentrated – whether it's atop the stem or circling it like a ring (if it's in a ring, skip to the bottom). If it's clumped above the stem, consider which of the following shapes it most closely resembles.

Anchor – If the sediment suggests an anchor, you're going to very likely have an unfortunate run-in with your ex. This doesn't mean it will be unfortunate for you specifically, but it might rile your current sweetie. Of course, this happens in small-town Sonoma more than most care to admit seeing as the dating pool seems to consist of only eight people at any given moment. Note, if the sediment you're analyzing was revealed while drinking wine with your ex, you've got more doubts about the future than sediment can reveal. Put the glass down, call Vern's Taxi and tell your partner you were with me (unless I'm your ex, in which case, call my wife, the Contessa, and have her pick me up.)

Sun – If the sediment is distributed with spirelike points radiating from center, this means you will soon be asked for your advice. If this is your first glass of wine, share your insights freely. However, sediment seldom appears in the first glass, which suggests you will be asked for said advice upon finishing your last glass of wine. In this case, you should also give the requested advice except you should do it with no regard for the person's feelings or any real consideration of the facts at hand. This is not your problem – they asked a drunk person's advice and you gave it to them damn it. Use phrases like "I'm just sayin'" and "I'm just being honest" and "Is there more wine?" I predict that embracing the moment in this manner will in the very least be entertaining until the tears come.

Ring – If the sediment in your glass appears in a ring around the stem it means that you're out of wine. What else? You will soon be drinking more wine. How can you be sure, you ask? You're in Sonoma, which means you're either at the beginning of a wonderful adventure – or the end.

Private Designs on Public Art

Though Sonoma boasts a statue here, a mural there, the valley's relative dearth of public art may account for an increasingly apparent faction of rogue artists who have come to fill the void.

Aesthetic renegades, Sonoma is their canvas, though the DNA of their work is a complex, and often controversial, double helix of graffiti and artistry. "Street art" is an oft-used term, though the work seldom appears on the streets as much as it does sprayed, stenciled, or wheat-pasted onto walls. That said, "wall art" suggests the generic prints hawked by Ikea for college dorms. If Théophile-Alexandre Steinlen had a franc for every "Chat Noir" print sold in the past decade, he could have hired a publicist so as not to forever be mistaken for Toulouse Lautrec.

The artists I've noticed effervescing around the fringe of the local scene won't have this problem. They don't sign their work, seeing as much of it has been installed illegally.

Consider the stenciled pseudo-mural applied to the rear wall of a building on the west side of the 500 block of Broadway. It's a fairly faithful rendering of both Michaelangelo's David and the Venus De Milo, applied in bold strokes of black spray paint in striking 2-D. In lieu of the fig leaves that sometimes accompany more modest depictions of these sculptures, bold censorial banners obscure certain parts of David and Venus' otherwise nude anatomy. Written on the banners is the word "Sensored," which I believe is a misspelling of the word "Censored." While in the throes of creativity, the artist apparently neglected the difference between a sensor and one who censors (one senses, the other is nonsense). Further confounding interpretation of the tableaux is the illustration of a surveillance camera focused upon the figures. I suspect the artist was groping toward an Orwellian-hued commentary a la Big Brother or at least Big Step-Brother: "I'm watching you – except for your naughty bits."

Perhaps the artist intentionally misspelled "censored," to suggest what techies call a "sensor deviation" which can result in a "sensitivity error" when measuring for various data. Unless Michaelaneglo's inspiration was not like the other boys, he probably endured a sensitivity error at some time or other, so perhaps here, the artist made his point – or not, as the case may be.

With both a nod to post-Beatle era John Lennon and Fluxus, the intermedia art movement, an interesting specimen of conceptual art recently appeared on the bulletin board at Starbucks.

Nestled within the clutter of visual white-noise advertising all manner of live music, yoga classes, and personal services, is a simple epigram in plain black and white: "Imagine – Imagine wonderful things, imagine a better tomorrow." The artist completed the instruction with a vamp on ye olde guerilla marketing technique of fringing a flier with pull-tab takeaways. Instead of the usual phone number, however, there is a reiteration of the "Imagine" message.

Cynics like your dismal columnist might find the enterprise trite, admonishing, or even vague. However, when I envision the artist – and I'm not being glib with the term here – strolling into the hurly-burly of a busy coffee franchise and sticking the product of their inspiration to the wall with little more agenda than to inspire a healthy moment of reflective Zen, I cannot help but forgo my snark and applaud the effort. In this regard, the piece is a success. How do I know? I sensored myself.

Leaf Blowers Must Die

Living in Sonoma during this time of year is like living in a postcard. Not the "Wish you were here" variety, which, in most languages translates as "neener-neener-neener," but the ones purchasable at the Visitors Bureau that depict our rural countryside, braided with vineyards in autumnal hues that would make every crayon in the box snap from sheer envy. Burnt umber? Ha! Take a slow northerly drive down Hwy. 12 and we'll see your "burnt umber" and raise you some "toasted sienna," "persimmon brandy" and "cinnabar blush" to boot.

And what sounds accompany Sonoma's November palette? The rustle of leaves, the wind's whistle through branches bare? No, a goddamn leaf blower, its stentorian belch ripping the noonday breeze like a chainsaw through a Monet.

I hate them. In my opinion, no object better exemplifies the worst of civilization than the leaf blower. Even the most grievous machines of mechanized death humankind has inflicted upon itself pale compared to the cosmic insult with which leaf blowers slur humanity. The guillotine and the electric chair at least do something. The leaf blower, by contrast, does only what its name implies – it blows leaves around. Sure, it seems harmless until one considers all the noise and air pollution and the use of fossil fuels – not to mention the money bled and blood spent in obtaining said fuel – and the leaf blower proves useful only as an instrument amplifying our ability to waste and ruin.

I mean, what's wrong with rakes and brooms? They've worked for millennia. What, are they too Amish? One should note that the leaf blower began its repugnant life as an agricultural chemical sprayer. Evil begets evil.

From the second story of my office building, I watched some idiot blow leaves from the sidewalk into the gutter for the better part of an hour. Why would I waste my time watching him waste his? The spectacle of Western Civilization crumbling before my eyes must be studied and recorded so that future generations might learn from our folly.

I asked the guy to stop so I could, you know, think. He said he would "when he was done." His verbal jujitsu notwithstanding, I knew I had him beat on at least one point. Whereas I at least appeared to be wholly human, he had obviously turned cyborg. A symbiosis had occurred between man and machine, an ergonomic pas de deux that found the man with a roaring motor grafted to his back and an arm affixed with a plastic snout that exhaled his humanity into eddies of leaves and dust. This sustained, bellicose, gaseous, thundering fart signified the utter futility of man in the face of Fall's grandeur.

By now, of course, the man-borg has deafened himself from an inner voice that once surely asked "Has it come to this? Is this the purpose I've found for my life – inefficiently blowing leaves into a gutter with a reverse-vacuum cleaner strapped to my back?"

The answer my friend is blowing in the wind, but it isn't blowing leaves around. This is what you should do with your leaf blower – liberate yourself from the machine, damage it irreparably, then use it as the basis for a homemade Boba Fett costume. I've seen this done before and it's awesome. Of course, to the leaf blower's acolytes, this is all just a bunch of hot air, to which I reply *blow me*.

The Car in Carneros

I'm a conscientious driver. Or at least I try to be, which is why, when my hands-free earpiece began to pick up air traffic signals and short wave out of Guam, I pulled off the road to take a call while cruising down Eighth Street East. I entered the empty sprawl of the Carneros Business Park where the sole building is festooned with a sign that reads "You Wanna Piece of Me?" which sounds more like an invitation to a bar fight than a pitch for some square-footage, but clearly they know their market better than me.

I completed my call – a tourism flak pal of mine had it in his head that the bureau must produce a zombie flick, you know, "for the holidays," and I was inclined to agree. Meanwhile, a small caravan of vehicles trickled out of the complex. When I finally attempted the same, I discovered the gate had been closed. Upon further inspection, including a firm tug of the padlock on the gate, I realized it would remain closed. My car and I were locked in an empty business park and night would soon fall. Yes, I'm an idiot.

I took a cursory tour of the complex in the vain hope that one of the cul de sacs was an inlet that returned to Eighth Street East. Nada. No roads lead to Rome here, let alone reality beyond well-manicured plugs of shrubbery and monumental signage. I was the sole human specimen in some botched recreation of my natural habitat. I was the existential punch line of a *Twilight Zone* episode.

It occurred to me to call the number on the "You Wanna Piece of Me" sign to invite the real estate agent down to kickbox or whatever and waylay him long enough to drive through the gate before he knew what hit him (read: speak rapidly in his direction – 200 polysyllabic words a minute, baby).

This plan could have worked had I not drained my phone's battery chatting about what wine zombies would pair with brains. The old iPhone car charger mysteriously will not charge the iPhone 3GS to which I had upgraded after literally dropping a call in a parking lot (damn that "butter fingers" app.) I was both trapped and unable to obtain outside help.

I decided I could either set up camp or circle the myriad cul de sacs again. This time around, however, I spied two blokes in the distance whose mise-en-scène recalled the set of "Waiting for Godot," simply, "A country road. A tree." To reach them I had to lurch my Mini Cooper over a cul de sac's curb and into a field, then navigate a minefield of ditches and detritus before reaching them at the other side of the wasteland. They were not impressed. Nor did they have a road to speak of, just a length of compacted dirt that someday might grow into a road. I rolled down the window and asked if the gate they had come through was still open. Here, I made two fatal assumptions: A) That there was a gate and B) that they had gone through it. The sun-baked men blinked back at me for a moment. Then, like Vladimir and Estragon, they admitted they could not remember. We gazed vacantly at each other for a moment too long. Then, I motored onward into the adjacent vineyard.

Fortunately, the Mini is no wider than the tractor whose dusty tracks I followed, turn by turn, in an attempt to wend myself out of the finely pruned rows of chardonnay. The cross-pitch for the motion picture version of this moment would be the *Italian Job* remake meets *Benny Hill* with maybe a little *Cannonball Run III* thrown in for good measure. This labyrinthine detour would have been a minor footnote to my day had it not taken an hour and half to finally chance upon a corrugated metal structure and with it the possibility of escape. There, two different guys stood gaping at me from a distance. This time, I skipped the dialogue and turned down yet another patch of earth with aspirations to one day become a motorway. The guys were having none of it. They leapt into a truck and "gave chase" as they say in the police procedurals. I pulled over.

"What the hell are you doing?" the driver asked.

I played dumb. "This is part of the winery tour, right?"

The guy snapped into customer service mode.

"Actually, no, you'll want to go straight and take a left, you know, onto the street. Where cars go."

"The street? Right. That would make sense wouldn't it?"

He nodded and with that I escaped to wash the terroir off my car.

Wine Shelter

At present writing, it's the 66th anniversary of the detonation of "Little Boy" over the city of Hiroshima. The event killed thousands and birthed both atomic warfare and the persistent threat of its existence since.

The fear of a nuclear holocaust coming to these shores reached its peak with the Cuban Missile Crisis in 1962, followed by a brief reprise in the 80s (Okay, class, raise your hand if you saw *The Day After* in grade school) and that WMD bait and switch in the aughts, which proved more a moral meltdown than a credible nuclear threat.

I can only imagine what it was like to live in Sonoma under the shadow of a prospective mushroom cloud – especially in the early 60s, when Father Still Knew Best and worshipped at the flickering altar of an RCA Victor television tube, "Wireless Wizard" in hand.

Picture a Don Draper-style pitchman, two fingers into his Gibson and advising television viewers about the efficacy of his brand of bomb shelter. Of course, if he were pitching a certain class of Sonoman he might well have opened with "Wine cave or bomb shelter? That's a good question. But when one is facing the annihilation of one's species, the better question is 'Why not both?'"

Meanwhile, at home, the emotionally absent man of the house turns to the subjugated mannequin he married and says "You know, dear, he has a point." But she's too hopped up on diet pills to really care about the bomb, wine, or even the man in the skinny tie who's always talk-talk-talking at her while she's trying to read the bodice-ripper tucked behind the Betty Crocker Cookbook. So, he lights another Lucky, leans in and is, in due time, sold on the wonders of the "Cellar-Savior, now in simulated wood-grain." As the spot continues, the pitch becomes more specious – "When you hold your tongue and say 'shelter' it sounds like 'cellar' doesn't it?" Or, "Gives new meaning to getting 'bombed.'" Sold!

Mind you, I haven't fact-checked this scenario with our local historians of whom there are two types – the professional, and those with a near-lethal blood alcohol level. The pros I respect enough not to bother with the inane query "Did a Sonoman ever have a combo wine cellar and bomb shelter?" But the provisional historians, the ones from whom "facts" come-a-tumblin' as if cued by the sound of a popping cork – they're ground zero for just the kind of hokum I enjoy most. Let's call this one Fat Man.

Brown bag, bottle, and bench – ask a drunk if he ever heard of a cellar-shelter and you'll learn all about the "Save Caves" of the early 60s and how he and his high school buddies used to sip Dad's wine and munch from tins of "Survival Crackers" and something called "carbohydrate supplement," which was just a fancy military term for candy. They called these boozy excursions their version of "duck and cover," which would probably be just as effective in the event of an atomic attack as actually ducking and covering. Which is to say, we're all gonna die so why not drink Dad's prized Lynch-Bages?

Forget Alain Resnais' *Hiroshima, Mon Amour*, it's "Sonoma, Mon Amour" in the dank and dark of the Amerian Dream. So, when the great portobello cloud blooms over wine country and you're snug in your Cellar-Savior, you can raise a glass and thank the man in the skinny tie. And the little boy from whence he came.

When One's Home is Another's B&B

Sonoma Valley's wine country is one of the most beautiful places on earth, which is why everybody, including your sundry friends and relations, want to visit all the time. Many of these folks, in fact, consider our homes their personal Bed and Breakfasts and will find cause to stay with us on the slimmest of pretenses. "The Wingo Regatta? Why not? Let's go to Sonoma and stay with our friends for free!" They don't want to visit us, they want to visit Sonoma – on the cheap.

Consider Rhonda S. whose college girlfriend suddenly materialized from the late 80s upon learning of her former dormie's 95476 zip code. The tipster in this case was Facebook where Rhonda absent-mindedly listed her actual city of residence not having considered that a cyber-stalker with whom communication had lapsed 20 years prior was looking for a place to crash after wine tasting. This is why all Sonomans using social media are encouraged to list their cities as "Guantánamo Bay." If some weirdo on your "friends" list still wants to visit you, encourage them to book a reservation with the Department of Homeland Security. You will never hear from them again. Here's the number (202) 282-8000.

Despite the fact that eluding the "transitory occupancy tax" culled by our local hoteliers contributes directly to the degradation of our city, many of our guests still insist on slumming in our spare bedrooms. Worse, however, are those who offer to "house-sit." These are people you should charge for the privilege of doing so. Fact: Several neighborhoods surrounding the Historic Sonoma Plaza are zoned for use as B&Bs. People who live in these areas are encouraged to hustle down to City Hall and file the appropriate paperwork ASAP because your relatives "have never seen wine country during harvest and thought it would be a wonderful time to visit." Splendid. Now, you can legally charge them. When they furrow their brows upon receiving your bill just remind them "It's the law." Call the City's Planning Division. Here's the number (707) 938-3681.

If a visitor manages to manipulate your affections such that they are now sleeping on your couch, be assured it doesn't take much to turn one's de facto hostel hostile. When encouraging an offender to leave your home an effective tactic is to bait them with their own misguided illusions of "wine country living." Tantalize them with visions of "Wine Cave Spelunking," which is similar to rappelling through a cavern but completely bogus. Your guests will look like complete idiots when they show up at the tasting room wearing a "seat harness" and inquiring which cabernet to pair with their carabiners. If the shame doesn't drive them away, then your evident cruelty surely will. Mission accomplished.

Of course, you can always make your guests history with "historical tourism." Send them to local history scholar George Webber, who, in the guise of General Vallejo, hosts an "Historic Sonoma Walking Tour," which he will lengthen, by $pecial request, to include such points of local interest as Petaluma. Here's the number (707) 694-5097.

If the above notions should fail, one's final course of action is to simply move away. Imagine the chagrin you'll inspire when some forgotten acquaintance passive-aggressively asserts their ignorance about local lodgings and you gleefully explain that you no longer live in Sonoma, but the Sonoma Valley Visitors Bureau could surely help. Here's the number (707) 996-1090. If you choose this rather radical solution, however, please consider that you must never return without a hotel reservation, lest you become one of them.

From Class to Glass – Online

I'm old enough to recall cutting school in the 80s and catching a television ad endorsed by on-the-wane celebrity Sally Struthers, as she hawked correspondence courses in such fields of study as "computer programming," "gun repair" and "high school" (which, upon reflection, reads like a prescription for "Columbine," but let's move on and spare Ms. Struthers an on-camera assault by Michael Moore.)

Of course, as a perennial n'eer-do-well and eventual dropout, the notion of taking "high school" via "distance learning" held particular irony for me since I lived mere blocks from the school (there's a metaphysical phenomenon here – the closer one lives to a school, the more unlikely it is that one will go there.) Moreover, why bother with Petaluma High School when I could simply ring Sally toll-free and "train at home for a better career?" Seeing as anything seems better than living the subplot to a John Hughes movie as a high school sophomore, I very nearly called Sally. I didn't. Apparently, no one did, which is why she eventually had to take the gig fronting for starving kids. Now that I'm a relatively educated accredited member of the media, I receive dozens of press releases daily touting means by which you, darling readers, may improve yourselves (impossible – you're perfect, I know.) A release came today, in fact, touting a new online course available from the University of California Irvine Extension:

"A Sommelier's Secret Guide to the Wine List: Wine and Food Galore," taught by the extremely credentialed Marlene Rossman, who certainly did not receive her various masters degrees and sommelier accreditation from the Internet. "This course takes the anxiety out of ordering wine from a restaurant list or buying wine in a store, which can be very challenging given the huge number of wine choices, both domestic and imported," explains course instructor and seasoned wine specialist Marlene Rossman.

Indeed, but this is Sonoma – where, if you don't make wine, you've probably written about it (it's like open-mic night at some rags, not to mention the local blogosphere – and power to us). If a Sonoman has any anxiety ordering wine it's because he/she is experiencing withdrawal and is preoccupied with the spiders crawling on his/her arms.

Now, I'm not criticizing the targeting of efforts of the PR firm (spam-shotgun aimed at lifestyle media – clearly it works), but I will suggest some additions to Rossman's curricula that will appeal to at least a few of my fellow Sonomans. Imagine Sally Struthers reading the following from a teleprompter:

Upon completion of the course, participants will be able to:

1. Uncork a bottle with your teeth.
2. Pair wine with more wine.
3. Pose as a critic to score samples.
4. Remove red wine stains from friends' clothes and carpets.
5. Do the ABCs backwards.

Of course, some Sonomans I know would slur, "Tell me something I don't know, Sally." But, theoretically, due to short-term memory impairment from a lifetime of imbibing, it's possible that such a Sonoman will end up taking the same course repeatedly with only a vague sense of déjà vino – the feeling that one drank some wine then forgot about it. I know I did.

Take a 'Nomaday'

I've heard Wine Country described as "Disneyland for adults," though I've never heard Disneyland described as Wine Country for kids. My inner child, the one who stole sips of Carlo Rossi Vin Rose when the parents' theater troupe wasn't looking, somehow resents this. Though Disneyland's adjacent "California Adventure" theme park makes an attempt with its "Wine Country Trattoria" decorated like a mini Sonoma County and boasting a wine list that would make Charles Shaw blush (that is, if Shaw made a rosé), both me and my inner kid prefer the real deal. Yes, I accept that I'll never be invited on another press junket by Uncle Walt for saying so, but alas, I'm not 8 years old, either. Besides, I live in the "Disneyland for adults" and seek my immortality whilst bobbing in wine, not liquid nitrogen.

The fact that Sonoma is the destination du jour for our thousands of annual visitors is somehow affirming, though it begs the rhetorical question, "If this is the place to be, why go anywhere else?" Given the current financial climate, we shouldn't go anywhere else. We should stay put and keep our dollars in local circulation. Having sidestepped my own economic downturn, which accounts for the recent move of this column (call it musical chairs, bed-hopping, or both, I'm no longer arranging deck chairs, which is a relief while assembling a crib), I can relate implicitly. Moreover, the marketer in me sees a bounty of opportunity. All we need is our own snappy term to make the place seem perpetually novel to ourselves. Consider the popular "stay-cation" (staying near), or "gay-cation" (staying near a same-sex partner), or the not-as-popular "hay-cation" (rolling around in a field). Forget the so-called "Che-cation" (putting your Che Guevera T-shirt in the laundry) and "nay-cation" (just saying "yes" all the time). We can do better, Sonoma. I suggest losing the "-cation" part entirely and plucking the suffix from "holiday," the Anglophile's synonym for "vacation" but redolent of lavender and Merchant-Ivory films. If your room with a view is anything like the one in which I'm presently writing – a garret above a light-industrial facility, sufficient for script to screen gigs and occasional runs to the taco truck – "going on holiday" has a certain ineffable charm.

To wit, I'm going to take a "Nomaday," a micro vacation that takes the "So?" out of Sonoma while contributing to the local economy. Here are some pocketbook-friendly notions for enjoying your own Nomaday. Sonoma and the surrounding area brims with Bed and Breakfasts, but it's difficult to justify the expense of an overnight stay when one lives here. However, if our B&Bs offered hourly rates, like the no-tell motels of yore, many of us would gladly visit for a little snooze and a snack. Call it a "Nap and Nosh" and watch the travel mags clamor for the inevitable "trend piece."

After your Sonoma-style siesta at the N&N, it's time for a spa treatment, but without the expense of either the spa or the treatment. Somewhere between a spa and schvitz, the Sonoma "spritz" squeezes an entire spa experience into a single, atomized spray, finished with a solid slap on the back to suggest the vague muscular soreness that follows a good massage. Of course, the same effect can be achieved by walking into any of a number of local taverns wherein a common salutation is a misty, beer-tinged greeting followed by a back-cracking bear-hug. Both are cheap and somehow therapeutic.

No Nomaday would be complete, of course, without sampling some of our local wines. Here's a tip – many tasting rooms waive their fees for locals.

For a deeper pour, drop my name. If, for some unearthly reason, my name isn't recognized, spare us mutual embarrassment by invoking a foreign accent. Should you be asked your country of origin, say that you're "from Disneyland." It's a small town after all.

Origin Myth

For each of us not blessed with being born natives of Sonoma there is a corresponding backstory to our arrival. An "origin myth," as they say in the screen trade. I've rewritten mine so many times I can hardly remember the facts, though I suspect this was probably my forgotten intention.

My backstory, so far as I can recall, had something to do with Los Angeles, a reignited romance and an unused return ticket. I won't waste ink on the specifics (we can catch up over a glass of wine sometime, if you really need to know), since my origin myth would scarcely rank a footnote in the Collective Annals of Sonoma Origin Myths, if there were such a thing. And there kind of is: I've been collecting local origin myths since I arrived in the fall of '05. I seek them out, tease them from casual conversation, bask in their backstories and catalog the dramatis personae.

These informal, informational interviews reveal all manner of motives, all hues of humanity in its pursuit of happiness. Every experience I've chronicled, no matter the circumstances that have shaped it, somehow affirms that Sonoma is one of the most brilliant places on earth, judging solely from the personalities it attracts and those it has retained (of course, I don't put my own name on this ledger, for at times I think it must be Greek for "dumb luck.")

There are sundry "made it big" stories, wherein the

protagonist decides to ferment in the wine country, something akin to an early retirement after achieving the necessary escape velocity from any of a number of prior careers (though there is a preponderance of technology and entertainment stories).

Each tale is compelling in its own right, as are those that have shared them with me – people who tend to give generously of their resources and themselves, adding extra burnish to the Sonoma experience. Then there are those drawn by the specter of opportunity, those who have recognized a burgeoning boomtown beyond the vines and epicurean escapades that underscore most weeks.

These deliciously hungry souls are easy to recognize – their furtive eyes very nearly glow as they pore over coffee-stained business plans in the corners of cafes, moving their lips in capitalistic incantations. Just as plentiful are the stories of lovers, those who followed their hearts to a particular someone, or just as common, to the town itself. But Sonoma is a tale of two cities: The one you're in and the one to which you're trying to get invited.

Though not terribly diverse or integrated, it is perhaps one of the few towns where a nouveau riche telecom refugee can discuss the corporate acquisition of local wineries with a recently transplanted Himalayan Sherpa and everyone gets along.

An area artist recently attributed this bonhomie to the fact that for many in the valley "work" is a mere hobby, often spiced with piquant notes of altruism and served on a crostini of civic duty. It's also a great excuse to drink. Hence the staggering amount of fundraisers thrown by the karmic-minded, which dot the social calendar the way phylloxera plagues a viticulturalist's sleep.

Despite this endless bacchanal – fueled by the democratizing elixir of fine wine and all order of locally raised, grazed, and otherwise-procured epicurean delights – there is a surprising lack of gout. This is just as well since it would interfere with one's early A.M. stroll home. Such constitutionals are highly recommended seeing as the town produces nearly as many DUIs as it does vino. Just don't pass out on the petanque court lest your nose be mistaken for a cochonnet and pelted with metal boules (though this can divert a hangover, it is considered rude to bloody the court and you won't be asked back.) The best bet is to take Vern's Taxi, especially if you're headed towards the outlands beyond the valley where the varietal of choice is meth and you ditched your bike while fleeing to avoid your patron's hubby.

Wince Country

Sometimes, wine country is "wince" country – as when one inadvertently refers to one's sommelier as one's "dealer." An acquaintance had me over to preview galleys of his forthcoming aeronautics tome and offered me a glass of wine. This is standard procedure when dulling the critical faculties of those of us in the media and particularly effective, I'm sure he assumed, when dealing with me – or at least my besotted persona, which I had left drying out somewhere before it could hang me out to dry. When I declined, the author insisted. "My dealer says it's a tremendous wine," he said. I raised an eyebrow and countered, "You mean your sommelier?" The author claimed he had said "sommelier" in the first place. I reiterated. He did the same. Awkward silence. I accepted his wine before the creeping chill in our conversation overtook the room as I gamely thumbed through his spaceship book.

When gossiping with a woman I know from the medical profession (tales of patient woe sans names, of course), she recounted a situation in which a client stated his preference to take his pain medication intravenously. When he was informed that "shooting aspirin" would be inappropriate in his case, the client admitted that he sought the needles so that he might extract wine samples through the corks of bottles stowed in his cellar. The doctor declined but was curious and asked why the man needed to sample the wine. "To taste the future," he said in a menacing tone, then slurped at his fingers for added drama before dashing out the door.

The above examples of wince country moments are, of course, not remotely representative of the typical local experience – an experience that I've come to adore for its beauty, bounty, and bonhomie. Nowhere on earth will one find a more hospitable and generous city. Everyone is welcome, including the occasional weirdo who, inevitably, will encounter me at some mixer or other and share moments best perceived through a glass, darkly. The hoary confidences I've accrued these past few years could fill a book (well, at least a slim book) and have always been fertile matter for this column. Though I don't necessarily invite these admissions, I do happily lend my ear because the best stories are often those that drift into the corners of parties, gather at the ends of bars and lurk in alleyways, searching, patiently, for an author. Moreover, it's my job.

Consider what happened when I was invited to a "cat party" in which everyone was garbed in feline drag and prowled the premises, occasionally sticking their painted noses into bowls of white wine. "Sort of gives new meaning to the much maligned wine descriptor 'cat pee,'" I joked, before being asked to leave because my cat costume consisted solely of a spiked collar slipped around my wrist. I was joined on my way out by another under-dressed invitee, who regaled me with tales of the pantomime horse party I had missed and how the equine halves departed in different color configurations from how they had arrived.

Last week, while shuffling down the bike path, I was entreated to drink with a pair of young men sipping from a bottle shrouded in a brown paper bag. When I declined, assuming the bottle they were nursing was filled with some noxious swill concocted to keep the fringe dumb and suppressed, they revealed it was a locally produced wine of splendid vintage that had received innumerable honors. I joined them and after a while realized, as my higher functions gradually became eclipsed, that if I were going to suppress the fringe that I too might bottle it in such a way that would appeal to ... but then the thought escaped me. It's all in a day's work in Wince Country.

Devolution

The Contessa was away on business last week, which provided me the opportunity to exercise an uncanny ability to transform any living space into a replica of my college dorm room. Dishes towered in the sink as precariously as a house of cards; laundry piles swallowed ottomans whole and balls of aluminum foil commemorated my nightly patronage of the taco truck like trophies to calories misspent. Under my watch, our quaint Springs bungalow transformed into a hovel akin to a demolition site and a crime scene, which by week's end lacked only the "caution tape." It also lacked me for much of the week given the week-long debauch photo editor Flash Lely and I embarked upon with the rationale that having worked nine to five, we should at least drink five to nine. Then there was the overtime.

Suffice it to say, Saturday morning, mere hours before I was to retrieve the Contessa from the airport, I had to rebuild not only my home but my life. Or at least render a reasonable facsimile of who I appear to be most days, before I became my own self-parody and dented my account at the Fig draining pintos (half pints of ale that I, ironically, imbibe at more than twice the rate of the standard issue pint.) Flash, a natural contrarian, drank Pimm's Cups.

Why is it that, in the absence of a mate, much of my male brethren and I devolve into lower primates? I'll leave that to the evolutionary psychologists. It affirms nothing of my sense of "maleness" to live like a shaved ape. In fact, it's contrary to every concept of myself I've heretofore devised. Please note the necktie. Yet, the moment my wife is out the door, I'm on the boat straight to Monkey Island. As natty a monkey as I may be, my impulse control in these moments is, of course, nil, which makes me especially susceptible to binges, be they pintos or, just as likely, movie marathons. No one needs to revisit (all of) John Hughes' films from the 80s in a single night's viewing, but it's been known to happen in my house, late at night. And it's wrong. James Spader in *Pretty in Pink* wrong, and I'm man (or monkey?) enough to admit it.

So, after sending a brick of red envelopes back to Netflix and rebuilding my abode, I decided to clean up, finally shave and begin working off the burritos on which I had been subsisting, all within the two hours I had before leaving for the airport to pick up my wife. I returned to the gym and contritely mounted what I have come to refer to as the "dreadmill." That my gym currently has two out of commission has been a point of some consternation for me seeing as, like theater seats, I prefer at least one between me and the strangers in my midst – for their sake – my social anxiety tends to make me chatty: "The palpable angst in this gym reminds me of that scene in *The Breakfast Club*, you know, like when Judd Nelson threw the lunchmeat on the statue. Don't you agree?"

While huffing, puffing, and generally ruing the fistful of cigarettes I had bummed earlier in the week, I caught sight of myself in the mirror, hunched, my wrists resting on the treadmill handrails. I realized that I looked like those illustrated depictions of ape evolving into man, except that I was about two iterations shy of walking upright. Indeed, I realized, there's more to being a man than the pose.

Nostrildamus Nose All

Unlike some of my pals, I don't need to walk into the local pub to get my nose whacked. I mastered the art of the self-inflicted nasal wound using that ubiquitous instrument of the Sonoma experience – the wine glass. How I transformed this delicate and otherwise benign vessel into an instrument of blunt trauma has little to do with the glass itself, but everything to do with the apparent enormity of my nose.

The Roman arch, as it turns out, is not limited to architecture – it's been fixed to the abutment of my face since the earliest of my days. Its genetic derivations remain something of a family mystery, though I once spied a photo of a camera-shy great-grandfather cowering behind a tree. At first glance it appears to be obscuring his profile. A second look, however, reveals that the trunk is merely camouflaging the bridge of his nose – I had mistaken the rest of it for a branch extending far out of frame.

Since transplanting to the wine country, I've learned to avoid certain types of glassware on account of my proboscis. Champagne flutes are a particular menace, since the mouth of the glass is too narrow to clear the tip of my nose. Thus, to sip, I must tip my head (and the glass) back about 75 degrees. The result is that I appear to be guzzling the sparkling, which, in point of fact I am, since the angle causes the wine to spill from the glass like a whitewater rapids. Likewise, stemware impresario George Riedel apparently has a grudge against those of us of larger endowment. Of the glasses he manufactures for specific varietals, it's only the wide-mouthed line created to showcase cabernet sauvignon that I can drink from with any ease (though I have to be mindful not to let my nose get wet.)

Due to a freak tetherball accident in the third grade, my nose lists a little to the left. This creates the optical illusion of being larger from certain angles, or rather, any angle except one. Through years of diligent study and experimentation with mirrors and other reflective surfaces (the reflecting pool at the Lincoln Memorial, say), I've learned how to counteract the effect by slightly cocking my head to the right. When I first spotted my future wife, the Contessa, I attempted this subtle corrective, but turned too far and inadvertently grazed my nose against a light switch, which momentarily dimmed the cocktail party we were attending. I tried to save face – or nose, as it were -- by suggestively chirping, "You know what a big nose means?"

"That you're a liar," came her retort.

Damn, the Pinocchio Reversal. Well played. I fell instantly in love. The Contessa herself has a fairly prominent nose, but its aquiline shape, even bridge and striking resemblance to Greco-Roman statuary amounts to a classic beauty and what some have commented is an aristocratic bearing. Mine just makes me look like a snob, seeing as I have to keep it fairly high in the air, counterbalanced by the long hair I've grown for ballast to keep my chin from crashing into my chest.

But tell us what happened to your nose, Cyrano, I hear you collectively cry. Okay, but you have to promise not to laugh. I was having a candlelit dinner with my wife on our back patio. After making a toast, I returned my glass to the table near a candle – too near, as it turned out. Later, I went for another sip, but the lip of the glass had become heated to the point that when it met the bridge of my nose (alas) a crescent shape was seared into it. And that's all I'm going to say about that.

When Terror Meets Terroir

This much we know: a somnambulist, conventionally speaking, is a sleepwalker under the control of another for what are usually nefarious purposes (see the murderous title character of *The Cabinet of Dr. Caligari.*) A sonombulist is the same as above, who lives in Sonoma. Often spied wanly wafting through cocktail parties or just as likely between taverns, the sonombulists come in every shade and hue of the social spectrum with concentrations toward the topper-most of the popper-most and the nethermost of the whatever-most.

If you've ever been at a function and suddenly snapped-to to ask yourself, "How in the world did I end up here?" you may be a sonombulist. At this juncture, I advise that you put down your drink and call Vern's Taxi (or, "for a good time" as it says on the paper's restroom wall "call Lenny.")

Sonombulism is not merely the result of over-imbibing, however; to many it's considered a state of mind – or lack thereof depending on how catty one's feeling. This is not meant as an insult – some of my best friends are sonombulists, which is why I'm always skulking around their parties.

The signs: If you're hosting a shindig and you find yourself asking "How in the world did Daedalus Howell end up here?" you're probably a sonombulist. If you're hosting a party and know how in the world I've ended up there, you're likely my puppet master and I'm your sonombulist. If you're not a sonombulist but received a call inquiring "where's the good time?" you're probably Lenny.

My gang (a loose collective colloquially known as "the cooperative," later shortened to "coop" and misspelled recently as "coup" in some watchdog blog rife with spurious conjecture about our intentions) worried we might have drifted into early-onset sonombulism when we tailgated the Blessing of the Olives at the Mission a few weeks back. Mimosas in hand, we loitered at the landmark in an attempt to jumpstart our holiday spirit only to realize what cads we had become. We should have brought mimosas for everybody. Sonombulists often forget the needs of others. The moment was sobering , but that was soon remedied by a visit from Gloria Ferrer.

Outbreaks of sonombulism, of course, run high during the holiday season and have for decades. I met a chap recently who recounted how his parents had attended a sonombulist party in the '70s and were asked to put their keys in a bowl upon entering. I suppose this was an effort to put the X back in X-mas as much as it was an attempt to curtail drunk driving. Since hearing the tale, my pal openly frets about issues of paternity.

"Listen, Lenny," I say, trying to sooth his jangling nerves, "it's not how you started but that you started. The rest is up to you, man. You can be anything you want to be."

"Even a sonombulist?"

"Why, yes, Lenny, even a sonombulist. Now, let's finish these mimosas before everyone else wants one."

"Mimosas?"

At night, as sleep drifts in and dreams beckon just beyond her pale veil, I sometimes spy the face of the lunatic who lurks within me, the nocturnal whisperer who encumbers my slumber with the simple command: "Dance, dance, dance!"

Yeah. I'm probably a sonombulist.

Surreal Estate

When it comes to local roadside attractions, Calistoga has a lock on the Petrified Forest (and the car-sickness it takes to get there); Penngrove's Gravity Hill remains the optical illusion of choice for teens en route to Make Out Point (where their own illusions about love and life are often dispelled on the back seat); the alleged Petaluma "River" (actually a slough or tidal estuary depending on the girth of your thesaurus) still astounds, I hear, neither ebbing nor flowing.

The Sonoma Valley, however, its landscape quilted by vineyards and surrounded by emerald hills, offers little in the way of natural wonders of the "Visit the Mystery Spot" variety. That is until an ad hoc consortium of neighbors on the 400 block of Second Street East devised some mind-bending optical wonders of their own.

Whether this effort is a conspiracy to siphon tourist dollars from that whole wine thing or just a coincidence drawn with a nod to M.C. Escher, the upshot is that there are at least two sights that astound and beguile, which I have added to my Sonoma Walking Tour of Un-Earthly Wonders.

Consider the home on the northeast side of the block, a stately home surrounded by the ubiquitous "white picket fence" of suburban lore. Now imagine a gate in that fence that opens to a path leading to the front door. A tableau worthy of Norman Rockwell, yes? Now imagine the relationship of the fence and gate reversed. There, like the lone first tooth of a toddler, stands merely the gate – but no fence. It beckons one to pass through it, if only perfunctorily, though one could just as easily, in fact more easily, go around it. The gate haunted me such that I couldn't muster the courage to investigate whether or not it was locked, though some dark part of me wanted to believe it was, if only to underscore the irony of it all. (Paging David Lynch – please report to the white courtesy phone – next to the severed ear.)

Down a ways, across the street, another sight for wide-eyes eerily awaits. The front of the house appears to be like any other of the handsome, early twentieth century properties that dot the block: its well-appointed lawn, the paint job tastefully executed and maintained. The diligent upkeep suggests a homeowner we would likely be happy to call "neighbor." A few steps to left or right, however, and one discovers that the homey image is merely a façade – the rest of the structure has been amputated just a few steps past the door. It's almost holographic – like my personality, the perception of depth is an illusion.

Unless one is looking for the anomaly, it's invisible thanks to our minds' "will to form." Though our eyes tell the brain that the image is woefully incomplete, the brain finishes the image in an effort to preserve its rather tacit hold on reality. When the brain finally accepts the bizarre notion that only part of a house exists (it looks like a Hollywood set), the resulting moment of disorientation qua revelation is vaguely pleasurable (like purposefully getting dizzy as a child, or inducing a head rush by hanging like a bat above a vaporizer filled with grain alcohol – don't try this at home, or anywhere.)

The mind can be rather willful when it takes umbrage with messages coming from our senses. This is why, for example, people think futons are comfortable when science has proven empirically that they are not, or that tofu tastes good when in fact it doesn't taste like anything, and that words arranged on a page must have meaning.

Labyrinth

"Labyrinth" – say the word to members of my g-g-generation and a Muppet flick starring David Bowie's worst haircut ever comes to mind (Spell the word and you can have my editor's job.) When classicists mull the labyrinth they recall Theseus venturing heedless through a maze, sword in hand, to slay the Minotaur and spare a few Theban virgins. Sonomans contemplating labyrinths (tell me I'm not alone) need not let their minds wander further than East Spain Street where a circuitous stone-lined pathway twists and turns and twists again under a ring of redwood trees.

Undertaken and overseen by the Trinity Episcopal Church, the labyrinth is a quick sidestep off the sidewalk and available to people of all faiths, including wine-drenched heathens like myself, who have trouble walking the straight and narrow and tend to confuse "cyclical nature of life" with "going in circles." That said, the Sonoma labyrinth rates well enough to be included in the Labyrinth Society's online "labyrinth locator" which lists thousands of labyrinths the world over (no, seriously). A question looms –Why would anyone willingly tie a 20-minute knot in one's daily constitutional?

"The labyrinth is a universal symbol of the pilgrim journey to the center of our being; it has no tricks or dead ends like a maze. One does not get lost- rather, this quiet walk leads inward," reads a sign near the roadside attraction, which also reminds that the hand-laid stone labyrinth is "a replica of the 13th century design found on the floor of the Chapter House in the Cathedral of Bayeux, France." Though environmental artist Andy Goldsworthy needn't fret about his job security, the stone and earth labyrinth does make for a fine stroll for the soul – rivaled only by the labyrinthine turns of the city of Sonoma itself, which can have the opposite effect on my soul.

For example, how is it the founding fathers named everything in the valley after themselves and their cronies but resorted to using the same numbers for the streets on both the east and west sides of the Plaza? Kindergarteners, whose wee minds amazingly contain letters and numbers, could have done better. One need not understand Cartesian coordinates to know that merely including the alphabet in city planning would save much tedious explaining to visitors.

Another labyrinth-like situation is the rather irritating fact that when driving one can only turn right onto West Napa from First Street West, likewise when approaching the Plaza from the south part of First Street West one can also only turn right onto East Napa. Confused? Me too. There isn't enough verbiage in all of geometry to adequately explain why this must be.

Moreover, due to never-ending street work at First Street West and West Spain (The Girl and the Fig has all but included "Dust Cloud" on their menu for patio diners) the northern part of First Street West can only be reached through Second Street East according to the ubiquitous crossing guard posted there who rejoices in chiding me every time I unwittingly attempt the turn. Somewhere in ancient Greece a labyrinth is missing its minotaur.

No Parking

On the 400 block of Church Street I spied a large note slipped under the wiper blade of a parked SUV. It read: "Why keep parking here, taking space from those who live here?"

The vehicle's driver had preemptively replied with their own handwritten rebuttal taped inside the windshield: "My manager says I can park anywhere on the street. Please feel free to call her (Valerie) at…" followed by the local phone number of a national video store chain.

Though I live nowhere near the 400 block of West Spain, have no issue with where this vehicle parks and clearly no business injecting myself into this roadside squabble, I have to admit to deranged opportunism that publicly displayed phone numbers arouse in me. It's likely the vestiges of having been a teenage crank caller – the skill set I developed serially dialing random numbers later found me a telemarketer through college and presently a newspaperman with a predilection for unnecessary phone interviews. This aural voyeurism is really just an acute form of curiosity, I've since rationalized, and a mindset I've found quite useful in my trade.

"Curiosity killed the cat," you chide.

"Ah, but a cat has nine lives and I intend to use them all in the name of truth," I wittily rejoin.

"That's not truth-seeking, that's animal abuse," you reply, admirably stretching the metaphor past the cat's pajamas (trumped, I retort by rolling up and smoking your paper tiger.)

After a dozen rings, alas, someone answered the telephone.

"Hello, [insert name of major video store chain recently sued in a class action lawsuit here].

"This is Daedalus Howell," I said, then paused for effect. "I write a column for the…"

"Hold please," the voice chirped. Ostensibly in show business, video store employees are apparently inured to celebrity.

A few minutes later someone was on the line again. I asked for Valerie and was startled to find I was speaking with her. "Damn, she's good," I thought, "I had the advantage of surprise and she took it from me like collecting late fees on the *Cremaster Cycle*." I nerved up and inquired about the parking ballyhoo. Valerie sighed.

"Any employee of any store here is not allowed to park out in the parking lot. So we have to find other locations. We're taxpayers, we can park on the street if we want to," Valerie said, ruing the neighborhood parking politburo.

"I couldn't tell you her name, but I know which house she lives in," Valerie said, which, in real life, did not sound as sinister as it does in print. After a beat, her thoughts turned back to letters her parking-challenged employees receive.

"You know, it doesn't work. You don't have to put a sign in your car that says 'My manager says…' You're an American citizen, you can park on the street, you pay taxes."

Inspired by Valerie's taxpayer angle, I decided that I too could and should park anywhere in an act of solidarity.

Ironically, when I tried parking on the 400 block of West Spain there weren't any spaces. Instead I parked on the Plaza and noshed at my cafe field office. A few hours later, I wandered back into the waning evening light in time to witness a member of Sonoma's parking enforcement leaving a note on my windshield. $25. Can I expense that?

Two Bottles A Day Named After Me Is All I Ask

It's common practice amongst writers to speed read their colleagues' work before entering a drinking establishment lest we run into each other and, running out of things to say about our own work, have to say something about the others'. This is how I discovered the notion of négociant-éleveur, which a local wine pundit made passing reference to in a recent column. The term refers to wine firms that trade in ready-made wines, which are blended and bottled under their own label. Brilliant, I thought, now my dream of becoming Francis Ford Coppola's Sonoma doppelganger can come true – I just have to finish a film and market a wine. Piece of cake.

Becoming a négociant, I thought, dovetailed nicely into my mantra "be the brand." Thus the wine would bear my mythological moniker. Being a writer I'm fairly good at selling myself, or at least my soul, so why not wine? Moreover, the label could have some clever spin on the Daedalus and Icarus myth. A gloss: Daedalus outfits his kid Icarus with wings of wax and feathers, chides him not to fly too close to the sun or else the wax will melt and he will plummet to his death, which he does because he's a stupid teenager. Family fun for classicists, but a bummer of a wine label. I mean, what's the tagline, "Don't drink and fly?"

"It would have to be something playful, but intelligent and sophisticated," explained Tanya Parmelee, a marketing professional currently fermenting her knowledge of the wine trade as a Ravenswood tasting room associate.

"For instance, your name is Daedalus, with our generation with all these layers of thinking and appreciation and what have you – if there can be a double entendre with the name – all the better. If it's someone intelligent, they're going to grasp what it is, for those that might only get the first level dimension of it – great – you won't scare them away."

This is what I suppose marketers call "spinning the bottle." I was game: finally I could get all the complimentary wine I ever wanted – whomever ran my wine interest would be a fool not to comp their boss, went the logic. If they didn't believe I was their boss, I would point out that my name is on every bottle. In terms of pronunciation, however, "Daedalus" has proven a very elastic name. It pulls like taffy, stretched hither and yon by word-of-mouth and gossip. Taking Parmelee's advice, I found myself suggesting pithy names like "Grateful Daedalus" and "Daedalus Man Walking," or, for those who prefer the long "A" vowel like myself, "Dae-Tripper" and "Dae For Night."

She was not as impressed with my suggestions as I was. She admitted that her initial association with my name was a video game. What?

"Remember growing up, our generation had 'Kid Icarus?' When I saw your name that was the first thing I thought then I started to laugh," she said referring to the mid-80s video game where classical and biblical mythologies are merged in a plot that has a wingless angel saving the world from Medusa.

"Hmm."

"But that's how marketers will think," Parmelee said plainly.

I thumbed my business card and notice that when I obscured the last five letters of my last name, the card read "Daedalush." Eureka! I mentioned this to Parmelee, who, laughing either with me or at me, eventually agreed that a wine named "Daedalush" might engender some Gen X cred.

"You have to make it as intelligent as possible. With Daedalush, you could go so many different ways," she said. "It's in enough of a window and haze of its own that people are going to wonder what it is…"

As Parmelee spoke, I began to percolate an even darker plan: instead of starting a wine label, why not simply print labels? I could run them through my home LaserJet and simply slap them onto bottles on store shelves like some madcap conceptual artist – a negotiant de sticker. Suddenly, it flashed before me, my first vintage: "Hello My Name is Daedalush." And wine critics everywhere felt a disturbance in the force.

Misconceptions about Wine Country Living

One of the benefits of having a presence on the world wide web is being accessible to a readership beyond the city limits of scenic Sonoma. Lately, their e-mailed queries have surpassed the usual "Is Daedalus your real name?" and "Are you single?" to those pertaining to life in the wine country. With 'Noma Pride, this week I attempt to answer their questions and disabuse them of their often charming misconceptions.

Q: If you put empty wine bottles on your doorstep do "winemen" pick them up and leave full bottles in their place?

A: Yes. Like the milkmen of yore, winemen retrieve the empty bottles from our stoop and replace them with fresh bottles of zins, cabs, and sauvignon blancs. Like their predecessors, these winemen also deliver dairy products like brie, manchego, and the stellar Vella Dry Jack. If you tip well, the winemen will let you ride in their rickshaws.

Q: Do the people who work at wineries also live there? A: Sometimes. Though colonial law has prohibited indentured servitude since 1670, many wineries have scuttled around the ban by defining work in the wine industry as a "lifestyle choice." In fact, most winery employees can leave anytime, but what's the point if your home planet is 100 million light years away?

Q: How can I tell if a wine is corked?

A: Look at the neck of the bottle – if the cork is still lodged within it, the wine is, as it is known in the trade, "corked." Similarly, if the wine is closed with a screw cap it's said to be "screwed." Hence the term "screwed up," which is colloquial slang for "empty bottle." For example, the bottle presently in front of me is empty, thus, "I'm screwed up."

Q: What does the term "terroir" mean?

A: It's French for "scary." Likewise, "appellation" is the Gallic term for "hillbilly," which stateside, of course, is no longer a politically correct way to say "toothless, inbred person from Appalachia." I understand that Sonoma County itself has 12 such appellations, but Napa County – clearly – has more.

Q: In a "barrel tasting" you don't actually taste the barrel, right?

A: Don't be silly, of course, you don't taste the barrel – that would be unhygienic. Instead, small shavings or "le snips" are broken off the barrel to be tasted individually. Of course, this is an archaic tradition that should have been banned years ago to prevent injury from splinters. As any winemaker will tell you, all barrels taste the same and contribute little if anything to the wine, but hey, if we can't respect another's culture, how can we expect them to respect ours when we take over?

Q: In a tasting room, when should one spit or swallow?

A: My advice to new imbibers is to always suck it up. A simple rule of thumb: If you are wine tasting – spit; if you are wine drinking – swallow. If the room is spinning while your head is in the toilet bowl – throw up. When you flush the toilet, pay attention to the direction that the water drains – it will be always in the opposite direction of your "spins" and will help balance you out. This is not "magic" as some people like to think, but a simply one of the many unexplainable phenomena of the universe.

Lifestyle Choice

A drawback to wine country living is the prospect of wine country driving. I'm not as cavalier as some I've witnessed making tactical chunders on winery roadsides, nor am I the type to hire a limo and froth like the garish bachelorette party toppling into the topiary at Gundlach Bundschu last month. (As Oscar Wilde might have said "The only thing good about driving drunk is arriving drunk.") So on nights out, the Contessa and I walk. It was during a stroll from Café La Haye to the bench outside (where we sat, trying to remember where we lived) that we spied a member of Sonoma's finest trundling from Rin's Thai to his squad car. His look was that of utter exasperation. Invoking my newspaperman's prerogative, I brayed repeatedly "What happened, man?" spurred by the Contessa's elbow in my ribs.

The officer explained that a thief had pilfered a bag of frozen shrimp from the Thai restaurant's freezers. All I could think was "Welcome to Slownoma." Bemused, I pressed the cop for more information and he reiterated: the culprit brazenly strolled into the restaurant's storage area, nabbed the crustaceans and vamoosed into the night.

"Did you get them?"

"No, she got away."

I later relayed this true-crime tale to my editor whilst

negotiating for this very column (I think I lost some ground by constantly referring to my "burgeoning media empire" and diabolically adjusting my inner monocle.) Presuming an interest in local law enforcement, his eyes brightened like a man about to sell another the Verano Bridge. He promptly offered me the police blotter, a hot potato in any newsroom, akin to penning obituaries, which I prefer, seeing as the dead are generally more forgiving of errata. I respectfully declined the police blotter (with gales of laughter), on account of my early-onset anti-authoritarianism, an affliction I acquired in adolescence when the police began to interfere with my joyriding.

This moment my editor, however, reminded me of a similar pitch I had been given by the editor of the *Petaluma Argus-Courier* when I first went legit as a newspaperman ten years ago.

Then a cub reporter freshly sprung from San Francisco State University's creative writing department (where I learned nothing about writing, but enough about financial aid to write a book about it had I actually learned about writing), I was offered one of two positions: "interim lifestyle editor" or the police beat. "Interim," I later looked up, meant the position was mine until someone cheaper came along. The police beat, however, I knew would be interminably dull seeing as there wasn't much to report since I had gotten my own car. Thus, I went for the lifestyle gig. Since then, I have tumbled through nearly a dozen affiliations in what we call in the trade the Comp, Pomp, and Romp tour.

In retrospect, had I braved the police beat, I might have acquired a taste for hard news, breaking stories and rooting through the small town dirt like a truffle pig after something like the truth. Ah, the proverbial Pulitzer path. As a lifestyle writer, however, the only prize likely awaiting me is gout. But, hey, it's about the journey, right?

Fortune's Stepchild

The freebie box in the foyer of the Sonoma Valley Library is a repository for the most unloved and unreadable books ever written. If these titles were worthy of being read, surely they would be shelved rather than moldering in a box, yes? Having been bargain-binned myself on occasion, I peruse these musty literary enclaves out of professional curiosity, which is how I discovered *Fortune Telling for Fun and Profit*. The title appealed to me because it speaks to questions key to the human condition: what's next and how much can I get for it?

Now, I've never been one for parapsychology. I have enough trouble with psychology in and of itself, namely my own, that I needn't spruce it up with a prefix. I file notions of the supernatural, ESP, palmistry, astrology, Tantric sex et al, in the portion of my mind that was vacated when the Tooth Fairy and Easter Bunny split town after trashing the place with memories of bloody baby teeth and unfound Easter eggs. I have little use for fortune telling – I've seen the movie, I know how it ends – but I have to admit, I'm always keen to have a leg up on the suckers of the world, I suppose from fear of becoming one myself.

As a shifty-eyed boy growing up in the SoCo suburbs, I dissected magic kits to reveal the molded plastic innards of their chicanery and knew, dubiously, that the purchase price of a child's soul was a two-headed coin. Likewise, I was enamored by the ads on the back of comic books that hawked wise-ass trinkets like hand-buzzers and X-ray glasses (which I finally purchased from the Tiddle E. Winks Vintage Five and Dime on East Napa a few weeks ago and promptly used to diagnose a hairline fracture in my denial mechanism.)

Such notions inspired me to become a self-styled con-kid, a proto-Ricky Jay, fleecing the neighborhood children with all manner of grade school treachery. I once goaded the gullible into putting their lunch money into a slot carved into a "magic" cardboard box I pulled on a wagon, out of which would tumble a ten penny tchotchke. In retrospect, it wasn't the prize that was worth the little handfuls of coins, but the experience of participating in something unexplainable and mysterious. It was a set-up that capitalized on my marks' need to believe. The box, of course, contained more kid brother than magic, but the con proved an object lesson in faith, which we know can fuel anything from rapture to war.

Fortune Telling for Fun and Profit was published in the mid-80s and a brief thumbing of its pages suggested the tome lived up to its title – but then titles aren't set in philosopher's stone, are they? A little online bibliographical research revealed that the book was originally published as *Fortune Telling for Fun and Popularity*, which presumably was too socially cloying for the then emerging "Me" generation. Besides, all a fortune teller has to do to win friends and influence people is to tell everyone how filthy rich they're going to become (which is rather like buying friends with Monopoly money, isn't it?)

For a moment, I considered absconding with the book and becoming a secondhand psychic myself, but alas, I can hardly divine my own next move, let alone some else's.

Later, I regretted forgoing the future and returned to the library to fetch the book. It was gone. My only recourse was what has come to be termed the psychic's salvo: muttering "I knew that was going to happen."

A Toast to Prohibition

December 5 should be declared a Sonoma holiday. This, the 339th day of the year, marks the anniversary of the 21st Amendment, which repealed Prohibition. Pop a cork – it's not that often the government returns a right it has wronged, let alone a right revoked with a constitutional amendment. In this case, the 18th Amendment, otherwise known as the Volstead Act, named for Andrew Volstead, chairman of the House Judiciary Committee (though it was penned by Wayne Wheeler and the Anti-Saloon League – a name, were it not for Wikipedia, I'd assume was a 1960s psychedelic band.)

For help imagining Prohibition-era Sonoma, take a peek into Plaza Liquors, which recently emptied its shelves of the demon-water due to a licensing ballyhoo that somehow involved a sting or police, or better, Sting and the Police, which means live music is indeed thriving on the square.

From 1920 to 1933, the powers-that-were enforced a national moratorium on booze, which led to oceans of bathtub gin, the invention of the speakeasy, and the inevitable rise of the mob (though a romanticized version of the mob has done good by those Hollywood artists whose names end in a vowel, generally, the Mafia is considered a bad thing – no offense Coppola, Pacino, DeNiro, Gandolfini, etc.) And locally, Prohibition led to the devastation of our wine industry. Prior to the amendment, there were 256 wineries in Sonoma County, but by its repeal, fewer than 50 wineries remained. Not until this year have winery numbers finally crept back to their pre-Prohibition peak. Yes, Sonoma Valley wine was once an endangered species; now one can't throw a tasting without hitting a negociant (just a wee jab for those who recall the brawl.)

If Sonoma's wine well went dry, we would be drowned by economic ruin, for our primary industries are wine and tourism – like one hand washing the other, with cash. So what are we doing to protect our industry and the precious 21st Amendment that again made it possible? In San Francisco, the aptly named 21st Amendment Brewery threw a "Repeal Prohibition Parade" on its 75th anniversary. The parade was led by two grand marshals, both celebrating birthdays – one turned 21 and the other 75. The duo was followed by the Green Street Mortuary Band, which I surmise, was meant to represent the death of youthful innocence and perhaps death from advanced cirrhosis.

Of course, Sonoma is no slouch when it comes to parades, seeing as we seem to have one for everything short of rain. However, Sonoma's 21st Amendment parade would likely devolve into a pub-crawl in a matter of minutes – better for the local economy as well as traffic. I considered supplying a map to aid in this endeavor, which I imagined would take place around the town square. Then I realized a "mental map" would suffice: Imagine a square. Imagine drinking. Proceed at right angles until someone comes to take you home. Wash, rinse, repeat.

As FDR quipped while signing the legislation that eventually repealed Prohibition, "I think this would be a good time for a beer." I quote those very words in FDR's honor every day. At about 3 o'clock. At about 6 o'clock I add "The only thing to beer is beer itself." Then I get cut off.

An American Sommelier in the Lower East Side

This is the penultimate day of the American Sommelier trade association's six-day "Intensive Napa Valley Viticulture & Vinification Course" currently being conducted in St. Helena. For wine-lovers without a professional interest in their passion, this might sound fun, the way "One-Hour Kama Sutra Training" sounds – at first. One can only imagine that the pleasure of such an immersing experience might eventually prove wearing if not, in fact, lethal. Combine the two in a death match of decadence and you'll know why Rome really fell.

Of course, those attending the intensive won't be "drinking" so much as "tasting," a point of distinction that would be lost on an attendee such as me, who declined an offer to audit the course for fear that both the learning curve and my level of intoxication would look like the proverbial "hockey stick" when graphed. And at the end of the course, my head would feel like the puck.

"Founded in 1998, American Sommelier is an organization dedicated to supporting the wine professional and to raising the overall level of wine knowledge and awareness in America through wine education" reads the backgrounder though there's nary a mention that it's headquartered in the heart of America's wine country – you know, on the Lower East Side of Manhattan. I suppose we should appreciate their attempt to honor our wine industry by hosting the class in Napa though it begs the question, why not Sonoma? Or more specifically, why isn't this event being hosted at Ramekin's or MacPlace or my house? Last I checked we have Americans and sommeliers in Sonoma (at this point, some reader will mutter "on the East side" and you know who you are.)

The short answer from the honchos in NYC would probably be "Um, where?" The long answer would use words like "prestige" and "provenance" though the P-word they really mean is "perception." Yep, thanks to that pact they made with Satan back in '76, Napa remains "top of mind" when anyone outside of our city limits thinks "California" and "wine" in the same thought.

Will Sonoma wines be represented in the so-called V&V course? Well, good question – as astute readers might have noticed this is the "Napa Valley" Viticulture & Vinification Course, which could mean it's all just Napa Valley wines. That said, beyond tutorials in "grape varieties, regulation and legislation, climate, geography, soil, industry statistics, the economy of wine and food pairing" the course will also present "beer, spirits, cigars, and blind tasting techniques." Okay, now this just sounds like a bachelor party. In fact, I'm surprised American Sommelier didn't just book this gig in Vegas. It would be like *The Hangover* meets *Sideways*. Hijinks ensue when four lovable wine stewards embark on a week-long wine intensive only to wake up with no memory of where they left their designated driver (Spoiler Alert: He's in the wine cellar of the Bellagio.) Make one guy a werewolf and we'll set the sequel in merry olde England, "An American Sommelier in London." Three glasses of red wine and the dude turns into a dog (this actually happens to me).

Perhaps it would be a waste of time to host an intensive

V&V course in Sonoma – everyone here thinks they're a sommelier anyway. It starts young – I once saw a kid make tasting notes on a juice box. By the time some Sonoma kids are in high school, they've pilfered so much of their parents' wine, they're practically oenologists (and under your breath you say "on the East side.") So, Napa can have its "intensive" six-days. Sonomans do it their whole lives. Can't handle that? Well, remember you can't spell "American Sommelier" without "I can."

Sonoma Dictionary

Though long-acquainted with journalist and fabulist Ambrose Bierce's lexicographical lampoon *The Devil's Dictionary*, it somehow never occurred to me to pen a similarly satirical *Sonoma Dictionary*. Until now...

Obviously, this is a long term project that neither this space (nor my deadline – or, ahem, fee) can tolerate in a single fell swoop. That said, there's no reason not to start and return as mutual interest avails itself. This is how Bierce himself did it – definition by definition in columns until he had the bright idea to aggregate them into *The Cynic's Word Book*. He then had the even brighter idea to change the title.

Among his definitions relevant to the Wine Country experience are "Wine, noun: Fermented grape-juice known to the Women's Christian Union as 'liquor,' sometimes as 'rum.' Wine, madam, is God's next best gift to man."

I'll follow Bierce's observation with my own:

Cabernet, noun: French for "Call a cab."

Corkscrew, noun: Any of a number of often improvised extraction devices for corks (spoons, pens, teeth; verb (slang): to win more than one's spouse's allotment of wine in a divorce settlement.

DUI, abbreviation, Driving Until Indicted: A

probabilistic maxim that dictates a drunken motorist may elude apprehension for an indeterminate period preceding their eventual arrest or death.

East Side, noun (slang): Where Sonomans who could not afford Napa live.

Napan: A palindrome.

Historic Sonoma Plaza, noun: A synonym of "town square" meant to arouse admiration in tourists; only public lavatory available after the bars close. Usage: "Please stand in front of me as I squat to pee on the Historic Sonoma Plaza."

Sobriety, noun; a neurological affliction that coarsens the perception of reality. Incurable but symptoms can be treated with regular consumption of wine. Usage: "Sobriety is the leading cause of boredom among Sonoma's teens."

San Francisco, noun: A city Sonomans ruefully mention but seldom visit. Related antonym: Petaluma: A town Sonomans ruefully visit but seldom mention.

Sommelier, noun: Person who spends another person's money on wine neither will enjoy; a waiter with a corkscrew.

Springs, noun (slang): An unincorporated area west of Sonoma inhabited by those who call themselves "Sonomans" but don't technically live in Sonoma; place where residents' sense of self-worth is in inverse proportion to the value of their real estate.

Vern's Taxi, noun: In Greek mythology, the ferryman who delivers the dead to the underworld.

Wine cellar, noun; a discrete space such as a closet, garage, bottom desk drawer or glove compartment, suitable for the storage of wine.

Pairings

Those in search of a wine country romance should forgo online dating and other matchmaking services and instead seek the services of a trained sommelier. Inasmuch as a good som might recommend a hearty burgundy to accompany your roast beef ("The astringency of the tannins cuts the viscosity of the fat," he wrote knowingly) he or she may also see merit in matching your love of lounging on the beach with, say, a potential mate's desire to bury their head in the sand. Ergo, if you can pair wine and food, you can pair people. I bet.

Soms know more than just wine. You've heard the expression, "Som guys have all the luck ... ?" Sure, that may look like a typo but it's really a pun obscuring a little-known fact: Sommeliers get laid. A lot. No matter if they're men or women, gay, straight – soms have it going on. No, it's not the size of their corkscrews or the fullness of their wine racks, it's because they are apothecaries of amour and wine is their magical elixir. Or as it might have been sung by a '70s glam band, "Pushin' the potion cushions the motion." And though that band never existed it should've.

Now, I'm not a sommelier, but I play one on TV, or at least on YouTube (okay, someone once rolled some video of me at a wine party and uploaded it to guarantee I can't go into politics.) The point is, I know wine through hard-won experience and I know matchmaking by enjoying as many matches as possible before getting flagged by the Centers for Disease Control as a "person of interest." This is why I'm more than qualified to aid singletons in their affairs de coeur. In Wine County, I've either slept with it or slept it off.

This much I know – opposites attract, until you've paired a sober person with a drunk. Then the attraction seems to be one-way. And always the wrong way. This is how it was explained to me by the girl with the "I Heart Sonoma" tattoo:

Prior to the sexual revolution, the pattern seemed to find a drunk man hitting on the sober woman or, worse, a sober man hitting on the drunk woman. Both are deplorable. Fortunately, a couple generations ago, gender equality and intoxication found each other making out in a coat closet. Since then, women have frequently gotten drunk and hit on drunk men, sober men, and even each other whilst inebriated. Thusly, the opportunities to find someone to hold their hair, whether that be while barfing or biting the pillow, are significantly up. And wine should be credited for its part *and often is*, later in divorce court.

As any sommelier-qua-matchmaker will tell you, wine is an aphrodisiac. But not for the same reasons that biochemists attribute to, say, chocolate. The neurotransmitters anandamide and serotonin, both naturally occurring in the seeds of the cacao tree are said to contribute to feelings of euphoria during sex. Wine, however, has only one active ingredient – alcohol – which lowers inhibition, judgement, and a general sense of good taste when it comes to selecting a partner. In short, if sex were a nation, wine is a democratizing force, the great equalizer and as potent a symbol of a mighty union as the American flag. Unless, you have too much wine, in which case your flag might be at half-mast and that's no fun — am I right, ladies?

Likewise, according to a 2005 North Dakota University study, drinking impairs depth perception. This accounts for many of the shallow personalities one might find in bed after a few bottles. This is why, when dating, my then-future-wife told me I have "holographic personality." Her perception of my depth was an illusion. Fortunately, being her husband has brought me new dimensions, like shared credit debt and the realization that everything I thought I knew about women is wrong. At least the other Wine Country husbands don't hate me as much now.

Which is to say, my wine and partner pairing strategy worked. As Euripides wrote, "Where there is no wine there is no love." To which we Wine Country folk reply "In wino veritas."

About the Author

Daedalus Howell began his career as a small town newspaperman, writing for the same paper he delivered as a schoolboy growing up in Petaluma, California. Later, he became a big city newspaperman, then a novelist and then a filmmaker before repatriating to his native Sonoma County, California. Presently, he writes and makes films in the San Francisco Bay Area where he lives his wife and son. He can be reached through his blog at DHowell.com.

CPSIA information can be obtained at www.ICGtesting.com
Printed in the USA
BVOW082013041012

302179BV00001B/1/P